A Time For Peace

A TIME FOR PEACE

Pacifism, Internationalism and Protest
Forces in the Reduction of War

PETER CALVOCORESSI

'To everything there is a
season . . . a time for war
and a time for peace' *Ecclesiastes 3*

HUTCHINSON
London Melbourne Auckland Johannesburg

This edition first published in Great Britain in 1987 by Hutchinson, an imprint of Century Hutchinson Ltd, Brookmount House, 62–65 Chandos Place, London WC2N 4NW

Century Hutchinson South Africa (Pty) Ltd
PO Box 337, Berglvei, 2012 South Africa

Century Hutchinson Australia Pty Ltd
PO Box 496, 16–22 Church Street, Hawthorn, Victoria 3122, Australia

Century Hutchinson New Zealand Limited
PO Box 40–086, Glenfield, Auckland 10, New Zealand

British Library Cataloguing in Publication Data

Calvocoressi, Peter
  A time for peace.
  1. Pacifism—History
  I. Title
  327.1'72'09   JX1938

  ISBN 0–09–167550–2

Phototypeset in Linotron Bembo by
Input Typesetting Ltd, London SW19 8DR
Printed and Bound in Great Britain by
Anchor Brendon Ltd, Tiptree Essex

Contents

PART I
Yesterdays

PART II
Today

PART I

YESTERDAYS

1

NO WAR:
The Sermon on the Mount

Natural history is about processes, human history ultimately about ideas. Ideas fluctuate in accordance with rules which, if they exist, have not yet been discovered. The future of mankind is therefore unpredictable and the past bewildering. Hence the peculiar fascination of human history. Although much that has happened can be discovered, the ideas behind the happenings – the way they arise, dominate and decline – are more difficult to track. Yet ideas rule. This book is about one of the most important ideas evolved by man, the idea that killing and war, which is multiple killing, are wrong. But whether war is the supreme evil or in certain circumstances a lesser evil than another – a sometimes justifiable activity – that question has never been conclusively answered. It has been accentuated by the invention of nuclear weapons which, by making it possible to kill more people more horribly and more quickly than ever before, prompts the conclusion that war and the risk of war have become uniquely and absolutely wrong.

It is reasonably safe to allege that at some point which we vaguely describe as the dawn of civilisation man began to give a high value to peace and to condemn and punish killing within his group and even within his species. Like walking on two legs this attitude to violence has been a distinguishing feature of the human kind. But whereas man has become very good at walking on two legs he has not become at all good at controlling violence, least of all at controlling the international violence called war.

Political evolution has accentuated this problem. As men congregated in societies, of which the dominant example today is the state, homicide too has developed politically. States have evolved techniques of varying efficiency to stop men from killing one another within the state, but they possess only rudimentary techniques for settling disputes between themselves without war. Peace, a moral imperative and a no less obvious dictate of common sense, has been and still is precarious. Two states may between them kill everybody, and since the forces for peace have not changed noticeably since the invention of nuclear weapons it is hazardous to gainsay the logician who maintains that they will. We live in the hope that a logician, however good, may yet be a false prophet.

Nuclear weapons emphasise the practical arguments against war: that war does the warrior more harm than good, that war does not pay. In the past the prudent warrior has had to choose his occasion carefully, for he is inescapably a gambler whose fortune (and his place in history) depend on how accurately he assesses the chances of victory and the value of what he stands to gain set against the cost of getting it. In these terms war is an instrument whose use may or may not be justified by results. The entry of nuclear weapons into the calculation has forced the warrior to see that the calculation is obsolete: war can never again pay and peace, once an option, has become a necessity.

But war has never been merely an instrument or option. It is also an evil to be considered in moral as well as pragmatic terms. The simplest moral attitude to killing – and so to war – is that it is in any circumstances wrong, regardless of its expediency. This is a view readily intelligible but far from universally accepted. A diluted attitude is that killing and war are *prima facie* wrong but not always so. This is a qualified condemnation of war which transfers debate to the question: what can justify war? Moral absolutes and moral certainties are dissolved in theological and philosophical discussions which produce compromises, the most influential of these being the doctrine of the Just War evolved by the Christian Middle Ages in Europe. In one form or another the idea that some wars are good and others bad has been the orthodoxy of our civilisation. But there have always been dissenters who have insisted that all war is irremediably wrong.

The absolute pacifist will neither kill nor sanction killing.

His god or his private conscience commands him not to and that is the end of it. He will not even kill in self-defence or in defence of his nearest and dearest; or, if he does, he will reckon it a human failing deserving censure along with sympathy. He will take no part in a war even if disobedience to the state's call to arms (or to other ancillary service) entails his own destruction. Like Franz Jäggerstätter, whose resolve is narrated later in this book, he is a convinced, often heroic and always lonely figure. He puts other people to shame but he shames few into following his example. His impact on human history lies in the force of personal example, a factor which is unmeasurable but clearly neither great nor nil.

More numerous but so far not much more effective are those who, whether inexorably or relatively opposed to war, try to minimize it by concerted action rather than personal example and withdrawal. This action takes varied forms. One is a multiplication of the personal refusal to fight so that there will not be enough people to do the fighting. This has never happened. Socialist dreams of withdrawing the working classes *en masse* from the state's command were crushed with pathetic completeness in 1914, while the British Peace Pledge Union of the nineteen-thirties was equally impotent. Another kind of action for the reduction of war works on states or governments rather than against them, elaborating schemes for leagues of states pledged to conduct their disputes without recourse to war. Such schemes, which existed in antiquity as well as in the modern world, have culminated in this century in the Covenant of the League of Nations and the Charter of the United Nations.

All these schemes equate war with the state and until the mid-twentieth century they recognised but tried to restrain the state's right to make war. But in 1945 the signatories of the U.N. Charter boldly withdrew this right and put the state in the same position as the individual in relation to homicide: that is to say, they outlawed war except in self-defence. This had never been done before (although it has been dubiously claimed that the Kellogg-Briand Pact or Pact of Paris of 1928 bound its signatories and adherents not to make war on one another). Those who signed the U.N. Charter did not imagine that violence and armed force could be eliminated from international affairs by treaty but they hoped to control and curtail the recourse to war by removing it from the individual state and legitimising it only when authorised and used by the community of states. This remarkable endeavour has, for reasons examined in a later chapter, so far failed to take root.

It is also, forty years on, under attack. It derives from the view that war is a disaster second to none. But this is not a self-evident proposition, even in a nuclear age. It is possible to argue, on the moral plane, that war is less evil than injustice, or that some wars are less evil than some injustices, and that therefore peace is not an absolute aim so long as certain injustices still exist. Furthermore the moral argument may join forces with the undertones of national self-interest and national fears which have hitherto been advanced and relieved by the sovereign right to make war; and morality may be further reinforced by a specific ideology which depicts an adversary as not only dangerous but satanic and so worthy of destruction. By a twist in the moral perspective war may once more be portrayed as a duty (like a medieval crusade): on the one hand communism, on the other capitalism, have mutually unacceptable faces which in some eyes justify holy war or even require it.

As the state reasserts its traditional prerogatives against an ambiguous and fragile international order, and as the temper of the times becomes heated by fearful new weapons and fervid ideological frenzy, on the other side the pacifist, whether a loner or in association with others, is moved to make his no less traditional protest. Peace and protest become one kin. But peace protests become unpeaceful.

II

We know little about Jesus Christ beyond the bare outlines of a brief life but we have a vivid impression of what he was like. This is the achievement of the four evangelists. St Paul, whose letters antedate the gospels, never met Jesus in the flesh and barely refers to him, while oceans of later Christian writing have done nothing to efface the portrait sketched by these first biographers. They present a teacher who – in the parables, for example – can be enigmatic but is never malicious or devious or, like so many subsequent Christian apologists, too clever by half. The evangelists were followed by medieval and renaissance artists who, in wood and stone, glass and paint, recreated the features of a man who was simple, calm, straight and above all good. It is a singularly concise and consistent portrait.

The most sustained single statement by Jesus that has survived (in a single extended version) is his Sermon on the Mount reported in chapters 5–7 of St Matthew's gospel. This text is also the principal source of Christian pacifism.

Although Christian churches and Christian monarchs have frequently behaved in the fiercer and more vindictive manner of Jehovah, the personal testimony and teaching of Jesus have saved Christianity from the moral condemnation it has too easily invited. Christian appeals for peace on earth still ring true.

Gods are not normally pacific and in this matter the god of the Jews was no better than the gods of Greece or Valhalla or India – splendid, no doubt, but capricious, cruel, unprincipled and narrowminded. They reflected warlike societies and gave lustre to atrocities: 'the Lord is a man of war' (Exodus 15: 3). Christendom has not been immune to this bellicosity but the life and example of Jesus, and Christianity's subsequent forced marriage with Greco-Roman civilisation, have endowed Christianity with an irenic strand which has persisted for two thousand years in a mainly hostile environment.

In the Sermon on the Mount it is not clear whether Jesus enjoins his listeners merely to abstain from personal violence or also to take an active part in suppressing violence; nor, in the latter case, whether the counter to violence might properly go to the lengths of counter-violence. The tone of the Sermon inclines to the more restricted interpretation. Jesus recalls and endorses the prohibition on killing, tells victims of violence to turn the other cheek and urges on them the seemingly unnatural feat of loving, blessing and doing good to their enemies. All this is addressed to the individual and to his part in a private quarrel. But there is also the blessing bestowed on the peacemaker, a phrase which has been repeatedly used as a text to commend an active role in tempering wider quarrels. Thus the dualities and ambiguities which confront the peacelover are already present in the Sermon on the Mount.

Present – but not at that time obtrusive. Christianity is a religion which, like Buddhism and Islam, is historical in the sense that it arose at a particular time and place. Christianity is peculiar in having assumed, wrongly as it turned out, that the time and place did not much matter because both were about to be extinguished: Christ's second coming and the end of the world were believed to be imminent. Besides, the early Christians were so few and lowly that the notion of taking a hand in affairs beyond the edges of their little groups occurred to none of them, except to the handful of missionaries like St Paul who were filled with enthusiasm to proclaim the marvellous Christian revelation. Keeping the peace meant abstaining from brawling in this transient world. Early Christianity therefore was conditioned by the circumstances of its formulation but convinced that these circumstances were of no account. There was no point in worrying about war if there was no time left for wars to occur. The issue could be neglected. If the world did not end, Christians would have to ponder their attitudes and behaviour to non-Christians, but they assumed that this future did not exist.

The world, however, did not end and, so far as Christians were concerned, that world was the Roman empire and anything but a peaceful place. The Christians multiplied to a point where their leaders must willy nilly (more willy than nilly) engage with that world and construct political attitudes as well as theological doctrines.

The first problem faced by Christians has lasted to this day: whether to obey the state when it required something contrary to their religion or their conscience, particularly when it required military service. This was not just a question of pitting the Christian creed against the demands of the non-Christian state, for the Christian creed was itself smudged; its pacifism was entwined with the bellicose elements in its judaic antecedents. If Jehovah demanded and led wars, St Paul and his successors were hardly less bellicose when they exhorted Christians to fight the good fight as soldiers for the faith. The symbolism of the two swords, one of them that of the Church, appears as early as the evangelical age (Luke 22) and before the first century was out the Christian church was described – by, for example, St Peter's immediate successor, Clement of Rome – as a militant body to be served as loyally as the Romans served Caesar. The church was likened to a camp and Christians, like members of peace movements today, felt themselves involved in a campaign. It seemed as though peace was for the next world and not for this unexpectedly persistent one, and in that case Christians had duties to others besides their communities of the elect. Jesus himself had told them to render unto Caesar what was Caesar's, and if that injunction did not extend to military service it at least implied the payment of taxes, which would be used to pay for wars.

A second problem was what to do about non-believers, lapsed believers and errant believers: pagans, agnostics, schismatics and heretics. As the Christian community expanded and became more closely organised its leaders became more political, more intolerant and more intent upon winning converts in this world by imposing the faith on the ignorant and the recalcitrant. Christianity was from its first days preached to the masses rather than the elite but beyond a certain point the masses might not be converted peaceably. Nor, once converted, did they always remain obedient – or pacific. Hence a division between a pacific but unambitious minority and a majority whose faith and fervour consorted ill with pacifism. In the ancient world the anchorite, in later times the dissident sect, held fast to pacifism at the price of abjuring the world or being rudely treated by it whereas the majority marched on, making the world more Christian but not more peaceful.

The nascent church had to avoid being trampled to bits by imperial persecution and being torn into pieces by its internal heresies. It could not afford to offend the state too seriously and it could not afford too much internal freedom of belief. It needed conformity and discipline, failing which it ran the risk of extinction. The conversion to Christianity of the emperor Constantine in the fourth century gave it security against the secular power on the one flank and strengthened its arm against heretics on the other, but in the earlier centuries it was unceasingly conscious of the difficulties of squaring politic conduct with its founder's principles.

Military service was a social as well as a religious problem. Christians were rather decent people but the soldiery were virtually a race apart, notorious for coarse and loose living, socially and morally near the bottom of the pile. The sort of person who became a Christian shrank from consorting with the sort of person who went for a soldier, quite apart from the Christian's religious objection to military service. Further the emperor was a rival god, even if not usually deified until after his death – he was served with sacrifices which were performed by officers and attended by rank and file and which were obnoxious to Christians, and by cult objects which usurped idolatrously the places reserved by Christians for their own religious symbols. For a century or so these matters did not cause trouble – or, if they did, we do not know about it. Christians were not wanted in the legions or allied forces because they were not good military material, but before the end of the second century they were under attack for refusing to serve. Celsus, a prototype of conservative pessimism, bewailing the collapse of the empire and its ideals of service, military and civilian, specifically attacked the Christians and their ideas for this deplorable state of affairs. He had no use for a religion which failed to prop up yesterday's values. Yet his attack reveals that a number of Christians were serving by this date (anticipating those Quakers and other pacifists who responded to the call to the colours in two World Wars). Tertullian (?AD 155–222) confirms the existence of Christian soldiers in the Roman armies but he disapproved unequivocally and insisted that a soldier who became converted to Christianity should leave the service. Donning Caesar's uniform in peace or war was in his eyes impermissible.

Tertullian's strictures made life difficult for the growing number of Christian servicemen. To resign on conversion was a hard thing for a poor man to do, although perhaps no

harder than staying on but refusing to kill as directed by
other eminent Christians. A generation later Origen (?AD
184–254) was no less outspoken than Tertullian against military service. He allowed that some wars were justified: Old
Testament wars had to be fitted into Christian theory and
were designated wars for survival and so permissible. But
Origen told Christians that they must reject any Roman
summons to serve. He regarded the state as a fundamentally
bad institution but somewhat confusingly held that it was
nevertheless not incapable of doing good, so that Christians
might contribute to its activities by prayers but not by arms.
Origen envisaged a gradual and universal Christianisation of
the world with the resulting elimination of war, but this
speculative long-term vision provided little present comfort
or guidance.

Both these eminent ecclesiastics upheld principles that
failed to command the assent of the weaker brethren upon
whom they were pressed. They restated the principle that
war was abhorrent because it entailed killing, but when it
came to practical issues of personal conduct their guidance
was ambiguous and unhelpful. Tertullian, a Christian
convert born in Carthage, a marvellously robust character
and writer, trained in the law and learned in Greek philosophy and science, much travelled in the empire, easily carried
away by the joys of verbal battle, ended his days – like
Tolstoy – outside the church and denouncing it. (He went
over to the heretic Montanists who deplored the corrupting
effects of the church's growing involvement in wordly
affairs.) Origen, born the Christian son of a martyred father,
was another to benefit from the Greco-Roman educational
system and an equally fiery champion of the virtues of primitive Christianity. He was an equal glutton for work, another
tireless traveller east and west of his base in Alexandria, a
scholar who wrote even more than the voluminous St
Jerome, the finest intellect of the early church, and the chief
vehicle for the confluence of Bible scholarship and Christian
teaching with Greek philosophy. Origen was withal a hard
man, chastened by meagre living and self-castigation. At
odds with his bishop he took refuge in Palestine where he
survived the Decian persecution (AD 250) by a few years.
Although, unlike Tertullian, he died in the church his

teaching was anathematized by a General Council 300 years later.

In temper these combative men recall the spirit of the Old Testament rather than the New. Like modern Bible Christians they are easier to admire than to like as they revel in controversy and pound their noisy way to righteousness. But their lives made a large mark on posterity, for theirs was the age in which Christianity survived and – even while still a small minority in the Roman empire – began to provide it with its intellectual elite.

Christianity was lucky in the date of its birth. The Roman empire furnished it with a common tongue (Greek), good communications between a network of fairly orderly cities, and comparative peace. These material advantages were no mean aid in assisting the Christian virtues and precepts to permeate a world which was spiritually undernourished. Neither the mystery religions nor the classical Greek schools in their silver age (Stoicism being now predominant among these) were for the many. The first Christian fathers pioneered Christianity into this populist gap while at the same time they laid the foundations of Christian scholarship, a development hardly foreseeable in Palestine or anywhere else in the first century. They also pointed Christianity towards the Latin-speaking half of the empire, notably to North Africa where, in an expanse of small towns and countless bishops, the first Latin churches were founded and Christianity began its transformation from provincial eccentricity to worldwide empire. They were very remarkable men.★

★ In purely theological terms Tertullian's historical importance lies in his hammering the last nail into the coffin of Gnosticism. The gnostics were elitists who stressed the value of *gnosis* (knowledge) as against *pistis* (faith). They claimed to know more and did. They assimilated Platonic idealism, the immortality of the soul, and belief in a hierarchy of angelic powers to form a *macédoine* of mysticism. Their world was not created by a god but by an inferior power and their magical knowledge was needed to combat the evil forces which had made and ruled the world. Their heyday was in the second century AD. Their defeat removed mysticism to the margins of Christianity where it has blossomed from time to time without ever returning to the centre.

2

JUST WAR:
The Christian compromise

The spectacular nature of these achievements of the early Fathers, without which we would not today be bothering ourselves about the Christian message, is larger in retrospect than it can have been in their own time when horizons were narrower and prospects seemed shorter. There was much humdrum work to be done in, for example, producing a textually reliable canon of both Testaments with critical commentaries and apologetics. The Christians still lacked the philosophical coherence and weight to pit against Greek and Roman paganism, judaism and mysticism. The early Fathers were brilliant drudges as well as travellers and fighters and it is to their meticulous pedantry as well as their fierce obduracy that we owe the preservation of the pacifism, the praise of peace, which they inherited embedded in the Christian message. Their followers had the problem of adapting this message which survived in, but no longer fitted, the world of which Christians were a part.

With the conversion of Constantine to Christianity at the beginning of the fourth century AD pacifism ceased to be a practicable doctrine and it became necessary to elaborate a new one. Constantine's conversion has not surprisingly been seen as an example of divine intervention in history. It was certainly a critical event, and was quickly followed by the conversion of many of the leading personages and families in the empire.

Constantine was a gambler. Like many gamblers he was constantly on the look out for adventitious aids to fortune and easily persuaded, when so favoured, that the gods had smiled on him. In 312 he invaded Italy in circumstances which would have kept a more prudent general away but his temerity was rewarded at the battle of the Milvian Bridge. He was a good enough tactician to sense that without something like divine aid his campaign should have been a failure. On the eve of an earlier battle he had seen the Christian symbol of the cross against the sun and had interpreted this sight as a sign that both Jesus Christ and Sol were on his side. This was a less bizarre conjunction than might be imagined, for the Christians were popularly supposed to be sun-worshippers, having recently adopted the sun's birthday as Jesus Christ's.

From this time, with one brief interlude under Constantine's pagan nephew Julian, the empire was officially Christian. The great persecution of Christians by Diocletian a decade earlier proved to be the last and Christians soon monopolised the principal offices, military as well as civil. At a Council at Arles in AD 314 the church (or that part of it represented there) declared that any soldier who discarded his arms in peacetime would be excommunicated. By the fifth century the empire's armies were wholly Christian and even clergy served in them, albeit rarely. Christians discovered the military virtues and the soldiers of Christ were not ashamed to become soldiers of Constantine's successors. The state ceased to be a regrettable evil and became instead an instrument for good, guaranteeing public order and private property (which Christians could now accumulate). Good too was the civilising mission of the imperial armed forces which were incidentally a great help in suppressing heresies – provided that the emperor was not himself a heretic, as sometimes happened.

War remained, however, a problem for Christians. Many, perhaps most, of them accepted the idea of a Christianised empire which fought their enemies; but some consciences were troubled. They were invited, by St Augustine for example, to renounce violence in their private lives but approve its use by the state. Their confusion was increased by a sense that it was no longer easy to say what made a Christian. The original characteristics of poverty, powerlessness and pacifism – the clearest attributes of Jesus and his first disciples – were no longer the touchstone. Very different kinds of people now called themselves Christian and were accepted as such. The extended Christian community was being pummelled by an awkward fact. The first Christians and their mentors (still revered) had set their Christian obligations by a personal refusal to kill or, through military or other service to the state, become an accessory to killing. They could do this without much embarrassment so long as they were too few to matter to anybody but themselves. When, however, they bulked larger in the state their doctrines became an offence and, like the peace movements of modern times, objects of suspicion, spying and harassment. Under these pressures Christian ideas and Christian practice shifted as, from the fourth century onwards, personal pacifism entailed a retreat from civic responsibilities which was no longer believed to be right. This pacifism was still in accord with holy writ and, when hazardous, noble. But it ducked the issue of war in a semi-Christian and Christianising world.

This issue became acute as the century wore on and it became apparent how far the Christian empire was in danger from non-Christian forces. Within a century of the conversion of Constantine Rome itself was sacked by Alaric and the pagan Goths. Before the end of the next century the Latin half of the empire completely collapsed.

On the one hand these calamities revived the view that the end of the world was nigh – not because the Goths were about to destroy it but because God would never have allowed them to get so far if He meant the world to carry on. (Indigestible turmoil produces apocalyptic reactions. A thousand years later the Anabaptists of Munster were equally convinced that they were present at the world's demise.) On the other hand the travails of the empire boosted the call to arms. Here was an emergency. In the period of the barbarian invasions of the west St Augustine (AD 354–430) summoned Christians to corporate militant discipline. By his arguments and his personality he created a dominant tradition, never erased in easier times and frequently renewed in critical ones – most decisively by St Gregory the Great (AD 540–604) who again asserted the authority of Christian institutions when there was for a time no empire in the west.

Augustine was born and spent most of his career in an African backwater which was nonetheless specially turbulent

and the focus for a special problem. After unsatisfying inter-
ludes in Milan and Rome, where his expectations were not
fulfilled – he seems to have been unable to follow St
Ambrose's advice to him that when in Rome he should do
as the Romans do – Augustine returned to his native Africa,
became ordained in the Christian church (which he had spent
some years attacking) and proceeded with apparently
genuine unwillingness to the episcopacy as bishop of Hippo.
In this Roman province orthodox Christians were outnum-
bered by the schismatic Donatists and the doctrinal conflict
between the two groups was sharpened by their difference
over how Christians should comport themselves in those
dangerous times. Whereas the Donatists wanted to remain a
sect apart in order the better to preserve the purity of the
teaching which they had inherited, Augustine insisted on the
contrary that Christians must venture forth for if they did
not Christianity would be extinguished and there would
be nothing left to preserve. Augustine was by nature an
expansionist who welcomed any opportunity, such as the
alliance of church and state, to extend Christianity to the
whole world; and in addition he judged that a forward policy
was imperative because the church was living in times which
offered total victory or total defeat. He is an early example
of the incompatibility of the missionary spirit with pacifism.

Augustine's imperishable fame comes first and foremost
from his superlative autobiography. The sources of his
influence are more complex. He was an exceedingly clever
and erudite man, with a lively mind, more open than
dogmatic, genuinely humble but capable of firmness in
decision and action. At first encounter he appears less
powerful intellectually than some other medieval celebrities,
but therein lay much of his enduring strength, for although
he schooled himself to become a learned man he conspicuously escaped that pitfall of higher education – which is to
be so conversant with the ideas and opinions of others as to
be hobbled in forming one's own. His ideas were shaped as
much by his surrounding circumstances as by his reading
and he changed his mind – and his religion – in response to
the impact of events and people. He lived in unsettled times
and an unsettled region, spending all but five years of a long
life in Africa where he was inescapably involved in religious

strife and national conflict. After his return from Italy, where he had become a Christian, he tried to live in a withdrawn community (something like the monasteries of a later age) but was forced to accept the responsibilities of a bishop, to battle against paganism and rival forms of Christianity, and finally to endure the siege of his metropolitan city where he died just before it was captured by the Vandals. All this instilled into him the omnipresence of violence and the necessity to fight back.

To Augustine violence, including war, was ineradicable. So the question for him, as a Christian, was how to place it in the world. He might condemn it utterly and refuse in any circumstances to allow it Christian endorsement; or he might define the acceptable occasions and permissible degrees on and with which it might legitimately be employed. He chose the latter course and became the most influential figure in the transformation and consolidation of Christian attitudes to war.

Augustine's reactions to the problems of violence and war were rooted in about equal parts in his theology and his pragmatism. This duality gave them, once he had made up his mind, great enduring force for him and for Christians for centuries after him. Augustine's conversion to Christianity emerged from a reappraisal of the nature of God. He had been a Manichee, believing that the world was governed by a ceaseless and roughly equal conflict between the forces of good and evil – between a god and an anti-god or devil. But he discarded this framework and became instead convinced that the world was made and ruled by an omnipotent and all-good God, whom he identified with the God of the Jews and Christians. The main element in this radical transformation was Plato. Augustine came to accept Plato's view that universals have objective reality: that is to say, that goodness, truth, justice etc. exist in something like the same way as a person or a tree or a table, only more so. He rejected therefore Aristotle's opposite view that universals have no real existence but are mental constructs derived from the perception of particulars. Augustine's acceptance of the Platonic view of universals led him to his belief in a supreme God embodying universal attirbutes and – partly in consequence – to a view of man as an essentially flawed creature. If God were by definition the sum of all absolute virtues, then man was in some measure inferior and defective. Augustine explained this defectiveness by man's original sin (he invented the term) as a result of which man could not be trusted to do the right thing even though, as God's creature, he had an inner striving to do it. Man needed both divine grace and firm mundane direction: illumination and discipline. Obsessed by the moral frailty of fallen man Augustine insisted on a strictly organised and supervised church (the word episcopacy means supervision) marshalled by bishops in their dioceses (the word for Roman military districts), in alliance with the state. Episcopal control was the way to defeat heresy, while the challenge from the barbarians must be parried by the state.★

Applying these beliefs to what he saw around him Augustine endorsed the church-state alliance which, in spite of numberless quarrels between churches and states, has remained virtually axiomatic for a millennium and a half in the main streams of Christianity, Eastern, Western and Protestant. His principal practical aim was to save God's church from disruption by heresies and extinction by infidels. The dangers were real enough. The violent excesses of the Donatists were even more vicious than the assaults of the Vandals, and however much he hated violence Augustine saw therefore no reason to submit to it. He did not offer the other cheek. Further, he admitted the use of force not only in self-defence and for retrieving stolen property but also in support of the state's function to reduce violence by keeping order. Further again, he welcomed the state's aid in repressing the church's enemies and would have been outraged by the argument that a Christian state – which was what the Roman empire had become – should not use its arms in this way. It followed that he reversed earlier Christian prohibitions on serving the state whether in civil offices or in the army.

Alliance of the church with the militant state was therefore justified, but it was also qualified. Augustine forged what became known as the doctrine of the Just War. If the church

★ Augustine triumphed over his Donatist enemies in the church of Africa but the state failed him when the vandals captured the principal cities of the Roman province in the year of his death.

were to endorse, even welcome, the use of the sword, there must be rules – rules governing the inception of war and its conduct. War was justified because there were worse things (the destruction, for example, of Christianity or simply allowing gross crimes to go unpunished) but nevertheless Christians could neither give blanket approval to the use of force as an instrument of the state nor allow that in war anything goes. The rules have been variously defined by different authorities at different times, but the existence of rules has remained a cardinal precept of all Christian churches and a necessary salve for their involvement in some forms of organized killing. Some Christian communities have demurred but so far they have failed to reconvert Christians as a whole to the pacific doctrines of the early church. If nuclear weapons do so, they will not be discarding Augustine's teaching but applying it in the new circumstances created by the advent of weapons of mass termination.

Augustine wished the church to bless the activities of the state. When in the next century the state disappeared with the eclipse of Roman authority in the west the church felt obliged to assume the secular power and duties which Augustine had wanted to bless but not to exercise. For a time the papacy under Gregory the Great and other Popes acted as trustees of the lay power, looking for somebody upon whom to confer it. The church, having sanctified the state's use of force, inherited it. Only with the coronation of Charlemagne in Rome in AD 800 could it revert to the strategy of alliance between church and state and so once more palm off the unpalatable business of warmaking onto the state. At the same time it elaborated a new doctrine – the doctrine of Just War which enabled it to draw a distinction between wars that were permissible and wars that were not, and in this way to ease the Christian conscience which remained true to the belief that all war was wrong.

In this transition from pacifism to Just War the fourth century AD was pivotal. In that period the Greco-Roman civilisation annexed Christianity which was transformed both in its material fortunes and in its spiritual values. This was the age when the church went public. At the beginning of the century (AD 313) Constantine decreed toleration for Christians, thus reversing Diocletian's policy of extermi-

nation and ending the series of bloody persecutions of which
the last (AD 303) was still fresh in the mind. At the end of
the same century (AD 391) Theodosius I went a long way
to giving Christianity a religious monopoly. Christians,
particularly those in authority in their church, faced a
dramatically changed situation whereby their relations with
the state which had emancipated them became paramount.
By a coincidence this question was sharpened by the
barbarian encroachments on the empire which threatened
both state and church and converted their accommodation
into an alliance.

The impact on the state was more obvious than profound:
it became in the course of the century explicitly Christian
(with some subordinate squabbling over which brand of
Christianity to adopt) but neither its power nor its forms of
government were much affected. On Christianity, however,
the impact of the alliance was fundamental because it raised
for churchmen the perennially insoluble equation between
spiritual and wordly values. The distinctive qualities of the
New Testament and of those – at first Jews but then also
Gentiles – who were creating out of it a new religion were
spiritual: peace and good fellowship were paramount and
were to be cultivated by spiritual teaching rather than
political arrangement. But when the church went into partnership with the state it adopted perforce many of the aims,
techniques and values of the wordly body politic – high
among them the pursuit of power and wealth by competition, conflict and war. That was a millennium and a half
ago, and throughout most of the intervening period the state
has been stronger than the church and has imposed its scale
of values on the society which state and church have, in
their several ways, governed. Only between the collapse of
ancient empire and the birth of modern state (c. AD
500–1000) was the church something like an equal or senior
partner. Before and since that period secular ideas have
predominated, particularly in the more recent epoch when
modern state, unlike ancient empire, has embodied regional
loyalties as distinct from universal aspirations.

The clash in the fourth century AD between the teaching
of Christianity and its worldly needs was experienced
personally by St Martin of Tours whose life spanned almost

the whole of this crucial century (316–397). Martin was a soldier from central Europe who became a French bishop and one of the founders of western monasticism. His father was a pagan officer who had risen from the ranks and he himself was sent off to join the army at the age of fifteen. He was baptized a Christian a few years later but remained in the army for 25 years. Thereafter he was increasingly drawn to a life of solitude and devotion but never shook off the calls of a politico-religious career, particularly after he was dragooned into becoming bishop of Tours. Martin lived, simply and uncomfortably, at Marmoutier on the Loire where he built himself an ascetic dwelling which grew into a monastic community. But he also laboured in the world, not only as a diocesan bishop but also through making appearances at the imperial court and by embarking on campaigns against pagans and paganism (in which he exhibited a certain ferocity). He tried to combine the offices of Christian pastor and clerical statesman; although irked by the flummery and pitfalls of courts he was aware also of the church's need to play a hand in the seats of power against heretics and heathen. His ambivalence was unhappy but not unfruitful, for out of it came the re-affirmation of Christian values in secluded religious bodies specifically created to preserve them in an unpropitious climate.

In the first Christian centuries this secession from worldliness had been made by anchorites and hermits who buried themselves in a desert or were pushed out of the broader Christian community. Martin's way of keeping pristine values alive was through detached communities rather than alienated individuals. His monks at Marmoutier and their imitators further afield kept their distance from the world in order to concentrate on enduring truth, while Martin himself, as both bishop and abbot, tried to have it both ways, dividing ecclesiastical life between a worldly church and an otherworldly monasticism. His attempt to resolve the dilemma of pacific ideals and bellicose realities was, however, only a partial success. It kept the ideals alive but was subverted when new and militant orders came into existence some centuries later and, by marrying monasticism with war, upset Martin's optimistic dichotomy. The crusading age, like the age of the barbarian invasions, sanctified war and threw up about a dozen new orders which were more militant than monastic. The most famous of these, the Knights of the Temple and the Knights of the Hospital of St John of Jerusalem,★ originated in the Holy Land to provide service for pilgrims – the former as a kind of traffic police looking after the roads and the latter as inn-keepers – but these humble beginnings were transformed when the crusading armies arrived and, having conquered the Holy Land, found themselves incapable of holding it. The members of these orders took the standard vows of poverty, chastity and obedience but they also became a fighting force, an extra army whose profession was war. Among Just Wars theirs were the justest.

So from approving war the Christian church in the west proceeded in the eleventh century to organize and lead it. The Pope became a generalissimo, mustering contingents and appointing commanders for grand designs; war became Holy War; and with the Crusades fighting reached a peak of popularity which it did not again attain until the rise of modern European nationalism. The circumstances were compelling, the intentions were respectable, the results miserable in both senses of that word.

The circumstances included a genuine spiritual revival, pioneered by the abbots of Cluny in Burgundy; a plethora of unemployed younger sons, dispossessed by the growth of primogeniture among the landed classes; and a cause – to secure for pilgrims comfortable access to the Holy Places in Palestine. This access was endangered by political rather than religious factors. The principal guarantee of peace and order was the dominance of eastern Europe and western Asia by the two superpowers based in Constantinople and Cairo. After many centuries of sporadic warfare the empire and the caliphate had espoused sensible policies of balanced co-existence, but this state of affairs was imperilled by the increasingly dangerous incursions of Turks from central Asia and Normans from the western Mediterranean which over-strained the resources of the two superpowers and led to a

---

★ Originally the patron saint of the order was St John the Almoner, an early medieval cleric, but with success the order welcomed the mistaken notion that it had been formed under the special protection of St John the Divine.

breakdown of public order, coinciding with an intensified western spiritual urge to visit the region and an augmented western supply of warriors available to pacify it.

It is easy in retrospect to decry the Crusades as land-grabbing homicide on a vast scale, but at the time the arguments for specifically Christian military expeditions seemed admirable. There was a dragon to be slain (there often is) and thousands of Christians took the Cross in a mood of generous exaltation. Nevertheless there was also another mood which had nothing to do with religious or moral values since the Crusades, however holy, could in no honest sense be described as defensive. They were aggressive wars which only an ideological casuistry could convert, in the language of the twentieth century, into legitimate collective self-defence.

Yet even then there were protests against the role assumed by the church and a fresh attempt therefore to curb what was being encouraged. There were peace movements among the clergy and laity which, then as now, restated pacific principles but did no more than that. There was a medieval prototype of the Peace Pledge Union which failed, however, to escape the paradox of recruiting adherents to fight against fighting. There were pleas to bar fighting on certain days such as Sundays and the main feasts of the church and even a proposal for a kind of long week-end which would have confined fighting to half of each week. None of these ingenious devices had any practical effect or did much to save the face of the nominally pacifist churchmen who found themselves constrained to take the sword or at least to encourage others to do so. In the crusading epoch war was neither condemned nor much curbed by the church; it was on the contrary taken over by the church which boosted the glorification of the secular warrior caste and promised rewards on earth or in heaven to those who rallied to the ranks or were killed in them. In compensation churchmen felt renewed need to regulate the forms of violence which they now sponsored.

II

The justification of war entails making rules about when a war may be begun and how it may be fought. This activity automatically entails, as a necessary by-product, a ban on some wars and some ways of fighting them – and a clean bill of health for others.

A ban may be absolute or relative, unqualified or qualified. For the best part of two thousand years Christian societies have on the whole taken the view that the use of violence in personal quarrels is not allowed: the question is not whether to prohibit it but how to eliminate it. The solution requires a degree of policing which, whether physical force is used or not, is a form of coercion and also provides rules and machinery for settling these quarrels without violence – the law.

The use of force in quarrels between states raises different questions because the analogy between the individual and the state, between a national society and an international, is incomplete. Time and the civilizing processes of disagreeable experience may render it less incomplete but at present the discrepancies remain more obtrusive than the similarities. In the general view a pacifist state is a contradiction in terms unless it is so weak that it has perforce no belligerent capacity or is comprehensively protected by a stronger state, while at the same time there is no practical way of policing or adjudicating the quarrels of major states which prefer an inchoate international system to a legal one. Pacifists who, in the first century or the twentieth, have tried to press the analogy between personal and state violence, and between domestic and international law, have been met with a number of arguments: that the state must have the right to defend itself because nobody else will, and the right to decide for itself when the need for self-defence has arisen; that the state is an instrument for the diffusion of law and civilized values which is enfeebled in the performance of these functions by pacifist propaganda, particularly if directed to soldiers; that so far as Christians are concerned the New Testament contains no explicit condemnation of war and the Old Testament much direct support for it; that pacifists are good people but naive and refuse to acknowledge that, like it or not, the world is not the kingdom of God on earth but something very different, a world where the bad have not yet been separated from the good or been subdued by them.

These arguments have enough in them to make pacifists uncomfortable and war either inevitable or a necessary instrument of last resort. The doctrine of Just War alleviates this discomfort. It asserts that war can be brought under discriminating human control so that, although endemic, it need not be unregulated; its inception need not be wanton or its conduct unduly horrible. It is an alternative to the wholesale denunciation of war as wicked and it therefore detracts from the absolute pacifist view and segregates those who take it. The doctrine of Just War is an example of the general proposition that it is better to strive for the attainable than for the ideal. There are good wars as well as evil ones, wars undertaken for good causes as well as bad, wars fought by permissible as well as illicit means, and so long as there are going to be wars anyway it is important to draw the distinction and find ways of enforcing them. Without the doctrine of Just War war crimes trials, which have been held in Europe since the late Middle Ages, would be impossible for there would be no war crimes. Against the doctrine the most potent objection is the ease with which it may be perverted, for example to justify the church's secular or missionary ambitions.

From Augustine's day to our own Just War theories have been a major scholastic preoccupation for churchmen and lawyers, moralists and political theorists. Restraining the incidence of war and regulating behaviour in war have been dominant themes, relegating to dissentient fringes the voice of the pacifist. But that voice has never been drowned and has gained strength in the twentieth century from two extraordinary novelties: the renunciation by the states which comprise the United Nations of the right to make war (except in very restricted circumstances) and the practicality of universal destruction by nuclear and post-nuclear weapons.

The definition of Just War has been fluid but the purpose unaltered: namely, to give some wars moral and legal justification and so place a ban on wars which lack this justification; and, further, to impose restictions on the conduct of war. The technical names for these two ventures are *Jus ad Bellum* and *Jus in Bello*. Medieval thinkers were more concerned with *Jus ad Bellum* than *Jus in Bello;* modern thinkers rather the reverse. This switch in emphasis reflects an increased acceptance of the incidence of war in the age of the secular sovereign state, both in its first phase as the projection of a personal monarch and in its later manifestation as the vehicle for national animosities.

The justifiable war includes a special subdivision – the Holy War. This is a war which, because it is commanded by God (or his plenipotentiary on earth) is *ipso facto* just; no question of its injustice can arise. The clearest, if not the most edifying, examples are the wars in the Old Testament commanded by Jehovah. They would today be described as genocidal.* But questions arose over the provenance of God's command after God ceased to speak directly with his own voice. Indirectness caused doubts and jealousy. The Pope, it was generally acknowledged, might declare a Holy War but when bishops claimed the same right Popes frowned on it. The crusades, blessed and directed by Popes, needed no further justification, although the finer spirits of the times were embarrassed by the manoeuvres of Popes who commanded princes to stop fighting each other in order that they might fight together in the Pope's wars. Christians were not alone in designating Holy Wars. Islam has its version, the Jihad, declared by a competent mouthpiece of Allah. In modern times President Reagan has lauded the fight against

---

* Jehovah created problems for Christians. In the second century the heresiarch Marcion denied that the Old Testament's Jehovah was the New Testament's God the Father. For going too far Marcion was declared a heretic. Such aspersions on the Old Testament contained an anti-semitic element which broke surface from time to time, e.g. Christian gratification at the destruction by Rome of Jerusalem in the wars of AD 67–71. Romans, although pagan, were cast as instruments of the divine purpose in exacting retribution for the execution of Jesus to please Jews.

the evil empire of the Soviet Union in language borrowed from the Old Testament (but with less evident credentials); the Ayatollah Khomeini and Zionists of the cast of mind of Begin or Shamir speak the same language as Reagan and Jehovah. In a secular equivalent of this divine scourge the Brezhnev doctrine asserts the right and duty of the Soviet Union to use force to maintain its version of socialism in neighbouring countries – i.e. to invade them in the name of holy writ – while American leaders cite a sacred duty to uphold democracy in Central America by open or covert war against unpalatable regimes there. Although the Holy War seems an anachronism, a similarly licensed sub-holy war finds favour in many places and, like the Holy War itself, dispenses with the limitations imposed both by *Jus ad Bellum* and *Jus in Bello*. The motto of the sub-holy war of the twentieth century is: Anything goes.

The pre-conditions for *Jus ad Bellum* were most clearly summarised by St Thomas Aquinas (1225–74). Thomas followed Augustine in wanting a central authority equipped and entitled to use force and with no squeamish reluctance to punish wrong doing and false belief. He also agreed with Augustine's judgement that the good of the community overrides that of the individual. Here are two of the profound differences between medievel and modern values: the equation of beliefs with acts, and the reversal of the relative importance of the individual and the group. St Thomas' Just War had three requirements: first, that the war must be waged on the authority of a sovereign. This left room for argument about who was a sovereign or how far down the princely hierarchy the right to declare war descended. Did the right inure in some or any feudal lord, or only in a crowned monarch, or only in the emperor? Secondly, the cause must be righteous. This condition meant that the act of war must be made in order to punish a malefactor who had recognisably committed some misdemeanor; but it was not necessary that the agent of retribution should himself have suffered from the misdemeanour. Anybody who satisfied the first requirement of sovereignty might act upon the second – subject to the third, which required that the intention must be pure. Purity in this context meant the absence of self-aggrandising motives. Further tests of the justness of war which were more strongly urged in later times include the conditions that victory must be assured in advance, which is to say that it must not be a gamble; and that efforts to avert the war had been made and exhausted.

Medieval interest in *Jus in Bello* was narrower and mainly related to the professional interests of the warrior class. In 1139, for example, a General Council at the Lateran in Rome denounced the use of siege engines and the crossbow (except against non-Christians) but this was as much a conservative as a humanitarian injunction: the knightly class had not yet used these weapons and was disdainful of them. The prohibition was in fact soon forgotten as new generations took to new inventions and, like Dr Strangelove, learned to love them. Equally flouted were attempts to halt fighting on Sundays and feast days. Knights were most interested in the elaborate rules about ransom but since these applied only to knights and not to all combatants they were only dubiously examples of *Jus in Bello*. In the later Middle Ages lawyers introduced a principle of proportionality, meaning that warriors must attain their ends without undue ferocity – an expression of distaste for what have subsequently been called atrocities. They also developed rules covering protected species: women, children, clerics, peasants and merchants received protection in theory and, more effectively, ambassadors and neutrals. Damage to civilian property was regarded as culpable but hardly to be avoided, and so classed as venial. Civilians should not be killed with intent but if they got in the way of battle that was probably their fault.

Such rules evinced a desire to humanize war and must have done something to tame it. Largely the creation of medieval ecclesiastics (many of whom were lawyers) they marked a considerable shift away from Roman jurisprudence which – in Cicero for example – regarded war as a legitimate exercise of the right to redress, to self-defence and the recovery of stolen property. But the Roman tradition was not lost. Isidore of Seville (?AD 560–636) succinctly defined a just war in classical terms: 'A war is just when, by a formal declaration, it is waged in order to regain what has been stolen or to repel the attack of enemies.' Here the essence lay in the relationship between the adversaries, the wronged and the wrongdoer. Augustine, by contrast, and his successors treated war as punitive, an enterprise to punish evil or eradicate error, a moral undertaking sanctioned solely by the behaviour of one party (the wrongdoer) and regardless of the relations between him and his opponent. Wrong doing created a universal right of chastisement rather than a particular right to retribution: the wrongdoer laid himself open to anything that might come to him from any quarter, a situation which – despite the limitations imposed by Just War – was wide open to abuse.★

This medieval view is akin to the modern doctrine known as the right of humanitarian intervention, equally open to abuse and at present out of favour with most jurists. It could be invoked to legitimize the use of force by any sovereign state to overthrow a tyranny (Hitler, for example, or Idi Amin) but it leaves the definition of a tyrant so vague that an attacker may, subject only to *post hoc* condemnation, proceed in arms against an inconvenient neighbour whom he chooses to describe as criminal: Hungary in Soviet eyes in 1956 or Nicaragua in American eyes since 1980 are glaring examples of this vulnerability of good intentions to partisan manipulation.

Augustine's religious and moral reasoning soon fell among lawyers. To begin with this was an unreal distinction since all learning was dominated by the clergy and laymen were not learned or even literate. But with the emergence of secular universities and the reanimation of ancient law schools in the later Middle Ages came a revival of Roman law as a distinct intellectual discipline, attempts to weld ecclesiastical (canon) law with Roman law, and the typically juristic insistence on the individual and his rights and the recourse to autonomous courts of law. The lawyers' upgrading of the individual is one of the principal marks of the transition from medieval to modern culture. With admirable pertinacity and the lawyer's love of precision jurists collected, examined and commented upon the textual heritage of Roman law in much the same spirit as the early Fathers had laboured over the texts of the scriptures. They

★ This universality of legal redress has very recently found new expression in a case in the United States in which an aggrieved foreign plaintiff got judgement against a tormentor even though the offences complained of had taken place in a foreign country.

hoped to reconcile the two traditions, Roman and Christian, to which they were heirs. The most influential of these intellectual gymnasts was Gratian, the author of the collection of texts with commentary known as the Decretum (published c.1140) who concluded that there were two types of legitimate war: just wars declared by a proper authority for a just cause, mainly self-defence or the redress of injuries; and holy wars undertaken to defend the church, promote Christianity and destroy heresy and paganism. Gratian and his successors were responding not only to their dual heritage but also to the politics of an age which divided authority between temporal and spiritual princes, the one keen to be allowed to make war to defend the state and the other to defend the church – defence being as liberally interpreted then as it is today. What the rules propounded by lawyers achieved was to set the terms for the arguments which an aggressor had to use when pleading that he was acting correctly. (A recent example of this perennial manoeuvring within the prevailing rules of the times was the British government's insistent assertion that the despatch of a fleet to re-capture the Falkland Islands from their Argentinian invaders was self-defence within the meaning of the U.N. Charter. What was significant was not the validity or invalidity of the argument but the trouble taken to maintain it.)

One of the purposes served by the Crusades was to paper over this crack between the temporal and spiritual powers. The existence of infidels and the wars against them enabled popes and princes to make common cause, at least on the surface, and to combine profit with merit. Infidels were smitten and princes enriched. The fact that both achievements were shortlived was not foreseeable and this disappointing outcome led to the shrivelling of a crusading ardour which was already something of an anachronism and fulfilled neither the requirement to recover goods nor that to avenge injury. Innocent IV, a great lawyer as well as pope, concluded that wars against infidels required the same justification as wars between Christians; but not so wars against heretics. The Albigensian crusades, besides being land-grabbing operations by northern against southern Frenchmen (and among southern Frenchmen), were a particularly brutal and nasty illustration of Christian malignity, rooted in a sense of insecurity prevalent in the thirteenth century and flaunting double standards which were to do the church much harm★.

The medieval church's attempt to regulate war was fairly laudable and pretty much a failure. The reality in the later Middle Ages was the growing authority of the secular sovereign state, escaping from papal controls, becoming a law unto itself, frequently at war with its neighbours. At the controls of these states were independent monarchs, a new breed of statesmen serving the monarch, and the embryonic art of diplomacy involving techniques for handling relations between states through resident diplomatic missions and *ad hoc* conferences. Out of this situation arose the practices and theories of international relations. An important part of the skills of statesmen consisted in having wars at opportune occasions and avoiding them when they appeared to be inexpedient. War was an instrument to be handled with care but not to be jettisoned.

The church failed in practice to keep control of war, so that the rules it made were largely ineffectual. It did not even keep control of its own members; bishops, for example, frequently went to war, particularly if they were also temporal lords. The distinction between wars against Christians and non-Christians, with the resulting licence to kill the latter or sell them into slavery on capture, was never an attractive moral proposition and became less attractive with better education. The arrival from the twelfth century of the lawyer-scholar, whose voice supplemented that of the theologian of the cathedral schools, produced more ingenious argument about the laws of war but also intellectual doubt about one of Just War's main props – the argument that a Just War was benevolent correction inflicted for the good of the peccant victim and out of love for him (similar to the modern schoolmaster's pharisaical tag: 'It hurts me more than it hurts you'). So two classes of dissentients, both of whom have their modern counterparts, began

---

★ The Albigensians were pacifist vegetarians with the exaggerated chastity which not infrequently goes with such inclinations. The virulence of the crusade against them is partly to be explained by the coincidence of their disruptive claim to be judge of their own doctrines with the threats to a scared Papacy from the Hohenstaufen empire.

to voice criticisms: professional thinkers (for example, Dante, Marsiglio of Padua, Erasmus) and fringe Christians (for example, Wyclif, Hus). Growing dissent preserved and revived the pacifist tradition.

3

Dissent

For Christians the collapse of the medieval empire in the thirteenth century was hardly less dramatic in its consequences than the conversion of Constantine. The Papacy, which willed the collapse out of its fear of the imperial power, was left as the sole symbol of the unity of western Christendom and was increasingly opposed by an array of vigorous princes instead of a pseudo-unitary but ramshackle empire. The ending of any notion of political unity in Christendom encouraged the destruction of religious unity by an alliance of secular princes with heresy. In the later Middle Ages the church was caught between its antagonism to the secular power and its dependence upon particular possessors of that power, the titular emperor being no more than one among these. The Papal attempt to maintain religious unity was negated by secular centrifugality; the Pope's dependence on princely support boosted every prince's leverage whether he was disposed to give it or withhold it; and the Reformation marked the failure of the Papacy to resolve the dilemma. The Prince and the state had won.

When the Roman Catholic church distintegrated at the Reformation western Christendom became divided into Roman Catholic zones (re-extended by the Counter-Reformation), established Protestant areas (mainly Lutheran or Calvinist), and a variety of dissentients whose principal common feature was their rejection of (and by) the new as well as the old establishments. The Roman Catholic church, militant for centuries, was made more militant by the schism. Of the principal Protestant leaders – Luther, Calvin and also Zwingli – none was a pacifist; the last two were markedly intolerant and autocratic while Luther, who began by insisting on the separation of church and state, ended by approving specifically Lutheran states and their use of force. Only the third group, the dissentients, were more pacific than not. There were, of course, pacifist individuals in all sectors, some of them impelled by their intellect at least as much as their creeds. Erasmus (1466–1536), an excellent devout Christian as well as one of the world's greatest scholars, was outraged by the decadence of Christianity, its fripperies and cheats disguised as pilgrimages and devotions. He saw a rottenness which conservatives refused to acknowledge and radicals saw only too clearly as an excuse for root-and-branch onslaughts. He looked back to pristine values and solid works, venerating not the bones but the books of the saints. Personally modest although sometimes spiteful, almost paranoidly fussy and fastidious, so timid amid the clashes of clerical choler that he struck a slightly lamentable figure, he was also a marvellously clear thinker and writer and a man of peace who deplored war both because it was un-Christian and because it was senseless, morally and intellectually repulsive. He travelled much and had a more extensive correspondence than anybody had ever had before. He has impressed generation after generation, has a place in the history of toleration as well as learning, but had no impact on the events of his lifetime: a sad exemplar of the limitations in action of the individual, however intelligent or good, or – to use language about to become current – of the subordination in politics of mind to matter.

The upheavals of the Reformation were superficially resolved by a territorial compromise by which each prince decided the religious allegiance of his state and his subjects. But this compromise did not end the fighting. For another hundred years wars were fought within states to determine the religious colour of its people, and national wars between states were normally given a religious coloration. Religious beliefs continued to command fierce and destructive loyalties and the period has ever since been characterized as the age of the Wars of Religion. They lasted until religious uniformity ceased to be regarded as an essential element in the authority of the prince.

These conflicts were a severe blow to the authority of

the churches. They perverted the doctrine of Just War by
harnessing it to sectarian or secular quarrels and by appropri-
ating the language of crusades to narrow and selfish aims.
The Protestants set a particularly grisly example with
Luther's injunctions to kill rebel peasants and John of
Leiden's violent establishment of the Kingdom of God in
one city with himself as King. Wars and judicial murders
were sanctioned in God's name by those who were certain
that they were God's servants and their adversaries the
devil's. Christian pacifism was even less evident than it had
been in the Middle Ages.

Pacifism nevertheless survived thanks neither to Rome nor
its principal opponents but to the dissentients who, in a
particularly violent age, held fast – most of the time – to the
precepts of the Sermon on the Mount. The terrible difficulty
of turning the other cheek in the sixteenth century was
exemplified above all by the Anabaptists.

Anabaptism arose in Zurich as an offshoot of the Protestant heresy of Zwingli who came next only to Luther and
Calvin as a leader of the flight from Rome. The essence of
Anabaptism is the need for baptism after the age of understanding, for which simple and not unreasonable belief the
Anabaptists seceded and were extruded from the Zwinglian
congregation. They were upholders of absolute pacifism,
determined to suffer rather than inflict pain, but their
pacifism was vigorous to the verge of violence and so
provoked anger and counter-violence from less radical Protestants. The Anabaptists insisted that government must
forgo coercion: the use of the sword could in no circumstances be justified, not even against the infidel Turks.
Although this teaching was perilously close to a contradiction in terms – what is a government that may not coerce?
– the first Anabaptists were able to embrace it because they
took a short view. Like the first Christians they were
expecting the second coming of Christ and the imminent
end of the world. But the majority of their fellow Christians,
more wordly, were horrified by this extremism and had no
compunction about resorting to persecution to eradicate such
dangerous and debilitating beliefs.

The Anabaptists dispersed from Switzerland to Germany
and then to the Netherlands. Persecuted in the towns, they

fortified their position among the poor peasantry, became a social as much as an ideological force and took a leading part in the Peasants' Revolt of 1524–25: they were social as well as religious radicals. The alarm and hatred that they inspired among the better off were revived ten years later when the city of Munster went over to Anabaptism under John of Leiden who ousted the prince-bishop, founded an anabaptist state with himself as king and in an excess of libertarianism took fifteen wives. His violent rule was violently destroyed in turn when he and his principal lieutenants suffered the barbarous vengeance of their fellow Christians. In the 1520s and 1530s thousands of Anabaptists were burnt and drowned.

Anabaptists elsewhere followed the irenic lead of Menno Simons (1496–1561, whence Mennonites) who preached discipline within the community but peace and toleration towards others. Renewed persecution during the Counter-Reformation induced many to migrate once more, others to modify their beliefs. Dutch Mennonites became in time pillars of the Dutch state and Dutch overseas empire, abandoning, together with German Mennonites, non-resistance to violence. A tougher strain moved to Russia but after the introduction there of universal conscription in 1874 could not permanently escape uncomfortable choices which forced them to compromise their beliefs. These Russian Mennonites were exempted from bearing arms but most of them agreed to give non-combatant service in peace and war; in the First World War only a minority of them refused actually to fight. Unhappy with these divisions 'and compromises some Mennonite groups trekked to Central Asia and North America while the descendants of those who remained in Russia were largely destroyed by Stalin who was suspicious of their German connections and classed them as kulaks.

The Anabaptists and other central European sects* were

---

* The Hutterites, an offshoot of Anabaptism, were expelled from Germany in the sixteenth century and reached the United States in the late nineteenth. Their founder, Jakob Hutter, was tortured and burnt alive. The migration of these dissentients shows that their physiques were as tough as their spirit. An even older sect was the Moravian Brethren, the puritan branch of the successors of John Hus who was burnt at the stake at Constance in 1415. Literal adherents of the Sermon on the Mount,

rooted in dissident, rejectionist attitudes, harking back to primitive Christianity and not initially forced by circumstances to accept the state as an inescapable part of the political scene. They were uncertain about the propriety of holding office in the state and paying taxes to it, less uncertain but not wholly so about military service. As countless pamphlets and debates bear witness, their study of the Bible failed to resolve their perplexities which were compounded as the state prospered and they themselves failed to find ways of living outside the state structure or evading its claims. They had to come to terms with it. But the erosion of their extreme pacifist and anti-authoritarian beliefs was not an entirely one-sided surrender. On the one hand it was partly a symptom of the growth of nationalism, partly too an application of egalitarianism which looked askance at a refusal to fight which transferred the burden and the risks to others; but on the other hand and most of all, it corresponded with changes in the state itself. The growth of toleration and of prosperity in the early modern period, and the first plans for an international system in which the state would be subjected to law, helped pacifists to moderate their antagonism to the state as such. So, later, did the extension of the franchise and other forms of participation in state business. For about two hundred years from the mid-seventeenth century the climate was more optimistic, a trend not reversed until the emergence of the aggressive nationalist militarism of the latter half of the nineteenth century and the invention of nuclear weapons in the twentieth.

The pre-eminent peace movement of these centuries from the seventeenth onwards has been provided by the Quakers, the English contribution to pacifism. The Quakers have won for themselves a remarkable reputation. They are regarded as both good and sensible. The implication is that they possess, and live by, high moral standards but at the same

---

wholly anti-war and anti-state, the Brethren founded an independent church but were all but obliterated by the defeat of the Protestants in Bohemia at the outset of the Thirty Years War. Having survived in secret they were resuscitated by the Saxon Lutheran Count Nicholas Zinzendorf und Pottendorf (1700–60) and rebuilt their organisation in Germany whence they spread to the United States, Great Britain and other parts of the world.

time see the world as it is and, eschewing flamboyance, labour in a practical way to make it better. Their conscience tells them to play a part in the world rather than abandon or condemn it, and they allow that others too have consciences whose dictates may differ: the test of conscience is not that it accord with Quaker teaching but that it be genuine. This bold acceptance of the primacy of the individual conscience has enabled them to escape from the trap in which St Thomas Aquinas was caught: St Thomas, faced with the question whether conscience was an ultimate touchstone of right thinking or whether a conscience might be wrong, prevaricated by concluding that the rule of conscience must be excluded from all questions of faith but should prevail elsewhere (for example, on participation in war). This ingenious quibble did not satisfy the Quakers.

The Quakers came by degrees to repudiate war (in 1661, to be precise, at a time when the restoration of the English monarchy gave a fillip to optimistic ideas, already in circulation, about man's ability to understand and control his environment, including the political environment). This repudiation was a general principle not easily acceptable in the seventeenth century when the idea of fighting for God seemed to be among man's higher duties – a principle adopted for a time by George Fox, the first Quaker. But soon all Quakers accepted the primacy of peace as a fundamental rule, thereby departing from the general puritan stock which sanctioned force in the service of reform. Quaker pacifism is both personal and general. On the one hand it is a personal response in an imperfect world, a response based on moral, religious and practical considerations. It proceeds, however, to wider things, analysing the causes of war and proposing schemes for reducing it. Even though preceded by international schematists like the Duc de Sully, the Quakers may claim to be the godfathers of the political approach to international peace as well as guardians of the individual's right to refuse to kill.

In their earliest days, under Oliver Cromwell, Quakers were turned out of the army because they were not wanted there. This contemptuous dismissal was converted into a positive refusal to serve which was maintained by a number of Quakers even during the patriotic fervours roused by

Napoleon. But not without penalties, social and legal. Forbidden by their principles to pay other people to serve in their place, Quakers faced harsh penalties, imprisonment as well as fines. But already their lawbreaking was regarded as different from that of common malefactors and their plight was alleviated when imprisonment for refusing to serve in the militia was abolished in Great Britain in 1852 and compulsory military service eight years later. How far Quakers should refuse ancillary non-combatant service has been perennially debated among them. The more rigorous have refused to work even on clothing for servicemen. Others have refused.to pay taxes: in 1839 a Quaker refused to pay rates on the grounds that the money would be used to pay the police force, and a century and a half later, in 1984, two Quaker women sought (unsuccessfully) to withhold a proportion of their taxes attributable to the defence budget. But the refusal to serve was never total. Quakers were enrolled as constables as early as the eighteenth century and in the two World Wars only a minority availed themselves of the exemptions granted to conscientious objectors.

The Quakers moved to the New World within a generation of the birth of their sect and tried in the non-sectarian colony of Pennsylvania to give a practical demonstration of the compatibility of their principles with the needs of government. They failed. The Spaniards, who preceded them to the Americas with a dose of Christian compassion and the doctrine of Just War, had not been prevented thereby from regarding the Indians as congenitally inferior or from fighting, pillaging and forcibly converting them. The Quaker approach by contrast was through negotiation but by the middle of the eighteenth century the Pennsylvania assembly voted for war against the Delaware Indians and the Quakers thereupon resigned from the assembly and gave up the governance of the colony. Their liberal principles lost them their power to insist on liberal behaviour. The history of this Quaker commonwealth was one of the obfuscation of an ideal and its failure to prevail in a world where British and French fought one another while Indians died in the *mêlée*.

This particular failure did not put an end to the Quakers' endeavours to fashion a more peaceful world. They, with other Christian minority sects, provided the core of the peace societies which flourished persistently in the English-speaking world in the nineteenth century and after, and they have bridged two streams of ideas: Christian moral teaching against war and practical secular attempts to get along without it.

II

The first of these peace societies were founded, independently of each other but roughly simultaneously, in the United States in 1815, to be later merged in a single movement. Their rules were moral, their purpose political. They opposed war on principle and argued against it on utilitarian as well as religious grounds. A slightly later comer, the New England Non-Resistance Society, founded in 1838 by Adin Ballon, the ancestor of modern American pacifism, with support from a variety of churches, was predominantly Christian and unbendingly pacifist; the American Peace Society, founded in the same year, was particularly interested in world government, international arbitration and other devices for the peaceful settlement of disputes. The first British Society of this kind was the Society for the Promotion of Permanent and Universal Peace founded in London in 1816, a few months after the end of the Napoleonic wars. Its chief inspiration was Quaker; its cardinal principles non-resistance to violence and total opposition to war, including defensive wars; its membership middle class, mixed religious and unreligious; its tone serious, scholarly and optimistic; its favourite implements popular education in a missionary spirit. All these societies contained a measure

of unfocussed idealism. Rising literacy, cheap printing and
a widening franchise were initiating the age of the pamphlet,
the public meeting, organised lobbies and propaganda, but
those who grasped at the opportunities thus created made a
painful mistake: they failed (as we shall see more particularly
in a later chapter) to appreciate the disconcerting fact that
popular feeling was not anti-war.

The peace movements were actively political. The London
Peace Society, for example, took a hand in the Anglo-American dispute of 1845 over the boundary between Canada and
the Oregon territory of the United States and sent delegates
to the peace conference in Paris in 1856 at the end of the
Crimean War. They staged, in London in 1843, a first international peace congress on the theme of the abolition of war.
It was attended by 292 persons from Great Britain, 26 from
the United States and six continental Europeans. The tone
of the meetings was both religious and businesslike and they
ended with a public meeting which attracted 2000 people.
The Society lobbied newspapers (which paid little attention)
and sent letters to over twenty heads of state. Such proceedings have since become standard. The sponsors of this
congress were British and American but it was followed in
1848 and 1849 by two more in Brussels and Paris – and
another in London in 1851 to coincide with the great Exhibition. The British continued to provide the bulk of the
participants, 670 out of 840 in Paris, where Victor Hugo was
the star and Alexis de Tocqueville played host one evening
in his capacity of foreign minister. 1867 saw the creation of
the Ligue de la Paix in Paris and the Ligue Internationale de
la Paix et de la Liberté in Geneva. The societies might feel
that they were getting somewhere, although the historian
can see in retrospect that what was coming was the Crimean
War.

In 1846 an American living in London made a novel move
by creating a League of Universal Brotherhood whose
members made a personal vow never to join up or help to
prepare a war in any way – a foretaste of the British Peace
Pledge Union of the nineteen-thirties. This unqualified and
personal stance was, however, not characteristic of the
national and international movements of the times which
were divided between absolute and qualified opposition to

war. The international meetings of the forties had majorities against all wars but significant minorities against aggressive wars only; these, however, were as difficult to define then as they are now – the intention behind the distinction obvious but an acceptable formulation virtually impossible. The American Civil War sharpened the confusion, presenting pacifists with an acute example of a classic dilemma: was war legitimate to extinguish slavery? On this issue, as on the right to secede, pacifists were divided. Among British politicians the most eminent pacifist or near-pacifist, John Bright, disclaimed opposition to war on principle but found grounds for condemning each war that came about (except some civil wars – the Canadian insurrection of 1838, the Indian Mutiny, the Christian risings against the Ottoman Sultan in 1876). Bright supported the Union in the Civil War, unlike most British politicians.

In the second half of the nineteenth century peace movements turned their attention more and more to disarmament on the assumption, which was to become central to anti-war thinking in the next century, that the scale of armaments and the arms race are themselves causes of war. They also persevered in their advocacy of international arbitration and other international procedures for averting war. But these political preoccupations never completely submerged the religious inspiration and personal moral commitment which were a stiffening force not far beneath the surface: as witness the American William Ladd who delivered 208 lectures in the United States and Europe in two years when he was approaching the age of 70, and Priscilla Peckover of Wisbech in England who founded a peace group and produced a journal *Peace and Goodwill* quarterly from 1882 to 1914.

As war becomes more frightful the history of peace sects and societies acquires a special interest. But in their own time these movements made little impact and were barely visible to the naked political eye. Perhaps their main contribution to what – few people disputed – was a good cause is to be found in a growing awareness that war may be bad for the winner as well as the loser. This was not a new idea: as witness Aristophanes, Erasmus and the *philosophes* of the Enlightenment. But until about 1800 the idea that a winner does not really win looked like an intellectual perversity, too clever by half. In the nineteenth century, however, it began to be a proposition worthy of closer inspection (and today it is a cliché), although with what effect on the behaviour of states and statesmen is still uncertain. In *The War of the Future*, published in Russia in 1898, Jean de Bloch expounded the view that war threatens the whole of civilisation. In order to press this case he had to portray the fanciful as factual and transpose nightmares into the rational light of day. Behind this essay lay a variety of forces slowly transforming the climate of opinion and among these forces were the peace societies. To say that they mobilized opinion would be a gross exaggeration but they were at least a ripple in a flowing tide. But towards what, if anything, was this tide flowing?

4

Peace by human contrivance

Almost as soon as the state became the dominant factor in public affairs, thoughtful people began to worry about the state's power over its inhabitants and its propensity to war with its neighbours. In Europe somewhere around the end of the Middle Ages invention placed at the disposal of state governments excellent instruments for keeping their citizens in order and for battling against one another. Other techniques – for easier communication over longer distances – were putting states in permanent contact with one another with the promise of frequent collision, whose natural outcome was war. These wars between states were different in motivation from wars against infidels or heretics and different in destructiveness from the wars between the princes and barons of the feudal age. The new secular sovereign found himself at an acme of power which was limited only by his finances, and this eminence ministered to his ambition, gave to victory in war a greater lustre than peace, and was nourished by the beginnings of popular acclaim (the origins of centuries of Anglo-French war are to be found in the Hundred Years' War for land and glory between English, French and Burgundian potentates).

The early modern age was even better organised for war, better equipped for it and better disposed to embark upon and sustain it. And all these aids to bellicosity were further boosted by the coming of the industrial and democratic revolutions which armed states as never before and put popular nationalist emotions behind state policies. The intriguing question of our own time is whether these revolutions are being transposed from the one side of the balance between war and peace to the other – whether military technology culminating (so far) in nuclear weapons is turning the popular mind more decisively against the use of war to settle quarrels, and whether reason and fear are creating popular anti-war movements with significant political weight.

In the alarming hurly burly of state against state, each armed by modern engineering and science and fuelled by chauvinist patriotism, the exhortations of pacifists and the example of saints or recluses, however praiseworthy, have remained futile. A different response has been the endeavour to prevent wars by organisation, arbitration and law: by human contrivance. If war may not be averted by moral precept or religious threat, by sage or priest, perhaps it may be averted by statesmanship. The essence of all such schemes is the acceptance of the sovereign state coupled with attempts to curb the exercise of its sovereignty. The authors of these schemes do not aim to remove the causes of conflict which they judge to be ineradicable, but they hope to provide procedures other than war for the adjudication of justiciable disputes and the resolution of political conflicts. They prescribe permanent associations or leagues of states with permanently binding rules (drawing on models from Greco-Roman times). They look to reason and sense, not morality, for they have been convinced – and believe that everybody else ought to be persuaded by reflection – that wars are terribly and demonstrably stupid. In this respect they have departed from the medieval tradition of dividing wars into the just and the unjust. While not disputing that some wars may be just they maintain that a just war does as much damage as an unjust one, agreeing with Aristophanes who, in three plays written about war during war – *The Archarnians, Peace, Lysistrata,* – argued that the mere waging of war is a self-inflicted injury and so folly.

Plans for securing universal and perpetual peace appeared in the seventeenth century and multiplied in the eighteenth.★ Grotius (Hugo de Groot, 1587–1645), the father of international law, accepted that a world divided into states was a world given over to inevitable and harmful wars. He

★ Medieval schemes, such as that of Pierre Dubois, do not count since their purpose was not peace but a Christian confederation to fight the Turks.

wanted to limit the harm. He put his faith in a two-track mechanism, an association which was to be international and regulatory, a league composed of sovereign states who would join voluntarily at the price of submission to the rule of international law. Grotius' insistence on law is a crucial step. Peace may rest on a legal order or on force. The Roman empire, as the Middle Ages constantly recalled, established peace but it did so by force and failed in the end to maintain it. Rome unified a vast area under a unitary military regime. Medieval popes and emperors dreamed of similar domains, spreading unity and incidentally bringing peace. Grotius, however, accepted political disunity and tried to show how peace might be secured without world government (what, on a restricted scale, de Gaulle meant by *L'Europe des Patries:* a Europe still divided into sovereign states but acting increasingly in concert through standing machinery). Grotius' plans required the voluntary adherence of sovereign states because he assumed the permanence of state sovereignty for the foreseeable future, and this voluntary basis of his international order required in turn that the volunteers should include all, or almost all, the states that mattered. If they did not, those outside the system would be unrestrained from making war. Universality was therefore complementary to voluntarism and all similar schemes up to and including the UN have rested upon the same duality.

Grotius was a clear-sighted lawyer with a statesman's pragmatic vision who, after losing the job of Swedish ambassador in Paris, died by drowning in the sad and false belief that his life had been a failure. He is the ancestor of our hopes of taming international society. His older contemporary, the Duc de Sully (1559–1641), was a career statesman with bifocal political vision who hovered between Grotius' voluntary universalism and a Roman peace to be imposed by his master, Henry IV of France. Sully's distinction is that he was the first practitioner in statecraft who, transcending the state, elaborated a 'Grand Design' by which he hoped to reconcile national interests and ambitions with international peace. His sketch of a permanent international council with an international headquarters and an international force is the ancestor of all later schemes with only one major difference: that, for Sully, international meant European since Europe was the universe in which the pioneers of internationalism lived.

The same was true of their eighteenth-century successors, of whom the most famous are Penn, Rousseau, Leibniz, Kant and Bentham. For William Penn (1644–1718) peace had become a supreme end in itself and not, as for the crusaders, an appeal for peace in Europe in order to concert a bigger war outside it nor, as in the mind of Leibniz, an aim only dubiously superior to justice. Penn agonised over the dilemma whether peace was a higher aim than rolling back the Turks from eastern Europe; he seems to have by-passed it by applying himself to the details of a permanent organisation for the preservation of peace and hoping that somehow the Turks and/or the Turkish problem would go away. But the Turkish problem – namely, how to fit a culturally extraneous element into an international community – has never gone away. It continued to perplex Europeans trying to operate a Concert of Europe in the nineteenth century, and although the Turks retained only a toehold in Europe after the first World War their place as an irritant was taken by Russia after the Bolshevik revolution, thus recreating the problem in the form of an antithesis between finding a way of living with communism and destroying it. (But with a profound difference: you can destroy a state and even a people but not an idea. For Penn the Turks were a physical anomaly in Europe, whereas anti-communists confront something which they cannot lay hold of.)

Penn, like Grotius before him and his eighteenth-century successors, faced a second problem which has remained unsolved. Recipes for peace by way of international organisation have failed to provide the international body with a way of enforcing its rules except, in the last resort, by the use of force, which in this context means war. The international body must either accept war as an ultimate instrument of state policy (as the League of Nations did) or divest states of the right to make war and assume that right itself (as does the Charter of the United Nations). In default of either of these alternative choices pacifists are left with the hope that a spell of international association and cooperation will usher in a rule of reason, if not of law; but optimists of this persuasion are not very convincing. The greatest optimist and the least convincing was Jeremy Bentham (1748–1832) who believed that war had nearly written itself off already by its evident senselessness. Immanuel Kant (1724–1804) was a more hesitant optimist, an optimist in spite of himself. He accepted collisions between states as a fact of life. He had no use for a superstate but envisaged a system in which states retained their independence and sovereignty but submitted to the overriding authority of law which they themselves freely and collectively would develop and define. Since this was the only way to peace he believed that it was likely to come to pass: the triumph of reason over war. Jean-Jacques Rousseau on the other hand (1712–1778) was pessimistic. From his various – and contra-dictory – writings on the subject he emerges as a rationalist who sees what has to be done but does not believe that it will be. He is honest but despairing.

With the nineteenth century proposals for international order began to advance from academic treatises to political drawing boards. Statesmen had been sufficiently scared by Napoleon, and by the new radicalism which appeared all over Europe on his heels, to toy with schemes for co-oper-ation which went beyond *ad hoc* diplomacy and shifting al-liances. If anybody was responsible for avoiding wars, then – in a world of sovereign states – they were. Blueprints for peace assumed that it was within the power of this narrow class of individuals to keep the peace and from this time onward the burden of popular and pacifist protest against statesmen has consisted of charges of failing to live up to this responsibility; it has regarded wars as testimony to bungling statesmanship.

But also to inadequate international machinery. In the last two centuries this machinery has been gradually improved. Since nevertheless wars still happen the improvement has been judged harshly and cynically (there have been some 200 wars since 1945) but this judgement has to be mollified by the impossibility of deciding how many more wars there would have been without the improvements which have been made.

The principal development may be categorised as either political or juridical, the one extending from the post-Napo-leonic Concert of Europe to the United Nations and the other embracing diverse ways of making international law broader, more precise and more effective. Throughout the period 1800–1950 wars, besides marking the continued failure of internationalism, have provided fresh impulses for devising better international machinery and more international law. This has been true of the Napoleonic wars, the Crimean and American Civil wars at mid-century, the Franco-Prussian war and the two World Wars.

The Revolutionary and Napoleonic wars covered the better part of a generation and were, by their savagery as well as their duration, as shocking to the sensibilities of the times as were the battles of the First World War on the Somme, at Passchendaele and elsewhere. One consequence was the attempt of victors and vanquished together to create a more stable and more predictable international order. The Congress of Vienna, which registered the end of Napoleon's plans for Europe and was followed for a few years by other international congresses (which today would be called summits, a figure of aspiration), raised hopes but the consensus and collaboration among the handful of leading statesmen quickly flagged, their separate concerns overrode their common purpose and they reverted to the practice of meeting after rather than in advance of crises. After the eighteen-twenties the principal European congresses were convened to make peace treaties in the wake of wars which the statesmen had failed to prevent (or in some cases had not even wished to prevent).

Revulsion from war was reinforced by the rapidly increasing benefits of international trade in a peaceful world – celebrated, for example, in the Great Exhibition in London in 1851 – but it was not until the next century that the international community adopted two crucial changes: the establishment by the Covenant of the League of Nations of a permanent international forum and the cancellation by the Charter of the United Nations of the state's right to make war. On the juridical front too there was much activity – the codification and enactment of international law, the extension of arbitration, the development of the laws of war, the proscribing of war itself – although the impact has been meagre because the law moves arcanely. *Eppur' si muove.*

As between states, the main instrument of international law has been and is the treaty, a quasi-contract between two or more states which, although sometimes expressed to be perpetual, is limited in duration.* Multi-party but still localised treaties became numerous in the nineteenth century, regulating for example traffic on the Danube or through the Suez Canal but avoiding more contentious issues or ones where mutual benefits were less obvious. The century was particularly enamoured of a special kind of treaty, the arbitration treaty. There were nearly 200 arbitrations between states in the course of the century and the spate of treaties accelerated in the next, but states jibbed at accepting compulsory arbitration and the most glaring gap in the Covenant of the League was the failure to insist on it. At the very end of the nineteenth century, in 1899, Tsar Nicholas II of Russia, improbably and with mixed motives, instigated the Hague conference on arbitration and disarmament. It was attended by 26 states and its scope was enlarged to take in the laws of war and the functions of the still comparatively immature International Red Cross. Besides banning gas projectiles, expanding bullets and the use of balloons for delivering weapons, the conference created a Court of International Arbitration. This was not a permanent tribunal, recourse to it was optional and possessed no sanctions, but it was convened *ad hoc* to consider 14 cases between its inception and 1914 and it was the precursor of the Permanent Court of International Justice and the International Court of Justice created in succession in 1919 and 1945. It gave arbitration between states a firm footing within the complex of international mechanisms for the peaceful settlement of disputes.†

---

* It is limited legally as well as pragmatically since the doctrine *rebus sic stantibus*, an implied term of the contract envisaging the constancy of significant surrounding circumstances, enables a party to it to plead that he is no longer bound because the circumstances have changed.
† A notable arbitration was that which settled the lengthy Anglo-American dispute of 1896–99 over the border between Venezuela and British Guiana. A more general Anglo-American Arbitration Treaty was rejected in 1897 by the U.S. Senate even though it excluded far more than it admitted. It was not to apply to cases involving national honour or territorial integrity or materially affecting foreign or domestic policies. An Anglo-French arbitration treaty of 1903 likewise excluded any issue deemed to affect national honour or vital interests. The earliest major arbitration agreement is the Jay Treaty of 1794 between Great Britain and the United States.

In the American Civil War the Union took the remarkable step of according belligerent rights to the Confederacy although the men fighting for it were theoretically rebels. The army's General Order No. 100, which was promulgated in 1863 and commanded proper treatment of the enemy, was a first step in bringing within the laws of war behaviour towards those not enrolled in the regular fighting forces of a state. A few years later the Prussians were notoriously brutal to French *francs-tireurs* in the Franco-Prussian war but an annex to the (rather vapid) Hague Convention of 1907 extended the laws of war to militias and voluntary corps upon certain conditions: that they have responsible commanders and distinctive badges, carry their arms openly and themselves conduct operations in accordance with the laws and customs of war. In the present century irregulars have played a substantial role in the Second World War, have been engaged subsequently in wars against the authority or existence of a state (most notably the PLO whose enemy is a foreign state), and have given rise to numerous conferences and proposals about their rights and the conditions to be attached to them. They have been acclaimed as heroes and reviled as terrorists – so indiscriminately in the latter case that the use of the word terrorism has become little more than a means to excite prejudice. The eighteen-sixties, which saw the insistence in the United States on humane treatment of enemies, saw also the first Geneva Convention (1864) on the treatment of the wounded and the St. Petersburg Convention of 1868 banning specified weapons. The wars of the nineteenth century had less effect on *Jus ad Bellum* but after the First World War tentative attempts were made to proscribe war: by the Geneva Protocol of 1924 which was designed to make arbitration compulsory but was not ratified mainly through opposition from the incoming Conservative Government of Great Britain; by the Pan American Conference of 1928 which renounced the use of war between American states; and by the Pact of Paris – the Kellogg-Briand Pact – of the same year whose signatories and later adherents also declared that they would not use war against one another. The legal effect of such declarations is debateable and the rise of fascism and nazism in Europe undermined the belief that war ought always to be foresworn, but after a second World War the Charter of the United Nations included at its very beginning a clear and legally binding renunciation of war (except in special circumstances to be considered below). The Charter thereby all but eliminated Just War.

Although the voice of the people has continued with some justice to blame wars on statesmen, statesmanship has made some progress over the centuries. It is not so clear that popular opinion has done so too.

5

War by popular demand

For most of recorded history what people at large think about war has been irrelevant. They have had no voice; wars affected few directly and not many more indirectly; those who did fight were professionals who adopted the profession of arms more or less voluntarily. But the beginnings of modern western democracy and of a popular press boosted *vox populi* and gave popular attitudes to war a new significance. This phenomenon, however, has not so far added much weight to pacifism. Wars have been approved by the popular majority (including members of peace societies), openly or tacitly.

This popular endorsement of war has gone hand in hand with a shocking growth in war's destructiveness. As successive industrial revolutions (contemporary with the democratic revolution) have armed the state with ever more efficient, more terrifying and more shocking ways of killing, the state's citizens have responded to this explosive brutality with chilling equanimity: repudiation of killing has not kept pace with the capacity to kill. War is not as unpopular as it ought to be and the question now is whether the helterskelter industrialization of war, culminating so far in nuclear weapons, has finally turned people against war and, if so, what they can do about it.

Democratic theory recognises the right of the people to share in power and democratic practice gives them a bit of it. In a parliamentary democracy this takes the form of popular elections, by secret ballot and at defined intervals, for the legislature and so an indirect influence over the executive branch of government. Further, it supplements this control by recognising certain rights of the citizen including freedom of speech and assembly, which are the essential ingredients of legitimate protest and made the people's wishes audible and visible. Democracy has given the citizen a much more restricted control over the third element in government, the judiciary: in the United States some judges are elected, in Great Britain and most other democracies none. Popular influence in the making of laws is therefore not matched by any equivalent influence in their interpretation and application: it is restricted to sporadic outcries against the more outrageous decisions or mistakes of the judiciary or police.

Democracy, however patchy in even the most democratic societies, has been an actuality since the earlier part of the nineteenth century and pacifists have not been wrong in ascribing some degree of power to the people. They have, however, been wrong in supposing that the voice of the people would be pacific. This illusion was not universal. Pierre-Joseph Proudhon in France, John Bright in England and William Lloyd Garrison in the United States were among the pessimists who believed that the power of the state, allied with the pull of nationalism, would abort schemes for the peaceful settlement of international disputes. The pacifists' enemy, the state, has been successful in getting the people on its side, even at its most bellicose. Where sovereigns exacted service by a mixture of loyalty and compulsion, the democratic state has enlisted popular fervour through nationalism, which is nothing if not adversarial. In England, for example, popular demand for war against Russia in 1854 was vociferous. The crowds which demonstrated for the despatch of an army to the Crimea were not themselves going to be part of that army but within less than a generation it had become impossible in most countries to demand war without running the risk of having to fight in it. Nevertheless the demand persisted.

At this stage militarism came to the aid of nationalism. The word itself, which appeared around the eighteen-sixties, has two meanings. It may mean domination of the government by the military openly or from behind the scenes, or it may mean the prevailing of militant attitudes whether in military or civilian circles. The first kind of militarism has been disliked by rulers as well as ruled at most times. Monarchs, whatever their own inclinations, have practical reasons for preferring as advisers pliant *robins* (men of the robe or gown) to robust captains, while civilian governments, democratic and authoritarian, have been no less anxious to distance the military from the seats of power and turn them into a salaried professional class confined to its special expertise. But this relegation of the military does not preclude militarism of the second kind, which is just as likely to infect civilians as the officer caste. The European nation state of the nineteenth century, and the nations themselves, became distinctly bellicose. The state possessed better engines of war manufactured in much greater quantity than ever before and the nations raged furiously against one another. The hundred years from mid-nineteenth to mid-twentieth century were the heyday of industrialised nationalism. Although the French Revolutionary wars began as an ideological contest, their Napoleonic sequel was an explosion of aggressive French nationalism which begat and polemicised other nationalisms in turn. After a pause, due to exhaustion more than anything else, war came back into vogue in the second half of the century, stimulated alike by victories and defeats: the Russians after losing the Crimean War and the French after their drubbing by the Prussians in 1870 were no less avid for war than the perennially successful Prussians. The social prestige of armies, hitherto low, rose and ordinary civilians found themselves diminished and derided for lacking the military virtues and martial bearing. The military did not seize power but societies were militarised by the transformation of civilian rulers and their subjects into military enthusiasts. All classes succumbed to a fascination with war and military machines, warlike games and pseudo-military disciplines (such as the harmless but telltale Boy Scouts). The nascent popular press fanned these breezes; and restlessness swelled the tide as populations exploded but ceased, towards the end of the century, to find relief in emigration or economic growth. In this apotheosis of nationalism pacifists were branded as unpatriotic, a sufficient condemnation. The miseries of battle and siege in the Franco-Prussian war, the squalid slaughter on the western front in the First World war and mass bombing in the Second sickened the soul but did not reverse the mood. Within the span of a single generation (1914–45) two great wars were fought, so destructive and so nearly universal that they raised the question whether this magnification of war might not kill war itself. The first did not and whether the second may, with the help of the fears implanted by nuclear weapons, remains to be seen.

The experiences of the first half of the twentieth century falsified some of the expectations of the preceding generation but the wars of this period – the Boer War, the Russo-Japanese and the two World Wars in particular – wrought other changes. There was very little refusal to fight but there were revulsions of a different kind.

The outbreak of the First World War was a particular blow to liberals and socialists who had imagined that war might be prevented by people refusing to fight in it. There were not nearly enough such people. The idea that popular power, even in a democracy, might shackle government or even in this case wish to shackle government was a grievously over-optimistic absurdity. Outspoken pacifists were, if famous (Einstein, for example), few and populist leaders were either not pacifist or without backing for pacifism.

In Germany a week before war began in 1914 socialists were demonstrating against war and proclaiming their intention to vote against war credits in the Reichstag, but when it came to the point they voted (with only two exceptions) the other way because they had come to realise that popular opinion was strong for war – the more so among the left wing lower classes because the main enemy was the hated Russian Tsarist autocracy. Even the mounting hardship of war and forebodings of defeat brought riots and mutinies but few recruits to peace groups; anger was directed against those who were doing well out of the war or conducting it badly rather than against the war itself. Socialists shrunk from opposing the war for fear of splitting their party: they prized unity above peace. Russian socialists, including Lenin, prized revolution above peace: they welcomed the war as opportunity. The French left performed the same somersault as the German and French peace societies collapsed; the socialist leader Jules Guesde joined the government. France, like Germany, experienced strikes and mutiny and a furtive resuscitation of the pacifist left but the spirit of war carried almost all before it. The Socialist International, which had been founded in 1889, disintegrated. In Great Britain five Liberal ministers resigned from the government but the Labour Party abandoned pacifism to the stouter but impotent Independent Labour Party. In the United States peace societies became converted to intervention by 1917.

But this catalogue of negatives is only a partial guide to the impact of these wars on popular attitudes. To take two examples only: in Britain recruitment for the Boer War disclosed the miserable physiques of many of the recruits and the horribly inadequate conditions in which they had been living, while the upheavals of the Second World War constituted a powerful ingredient in the social reforms of mid-century. In Russia the humiliations and incompetence of the Russo-Japanese and First World War sharpened hostility to the Tsarist autocracy and fuelled the revolutions of 1917. War therefore had considerable effect. But owing largely to the continuing strength of national feelings and habits the effects were national rather than international. The revulsions were against conditions within the state rather than against the wars conducted by it, and the cry for fairness at home was louder than the cry for peace abroad.

II

Within a special area, limited but important, the First World War marked an advance which was held and developed in the Second. This concerned the right of the individual conscientious objector to refuse the call to serve the state at war.

The admission of this right is a step forwards in the history of toleration. In modern Europe, since the Renaissance, toleration began as religious toleration. It was a secular reaction against religious intolerance and was fuelled by religious wars and their murderous consequences. It was intellectual inasmuch as it denounced the stupidity of destruction, moral inasmuch as it proclaimed freedom of conscience and belief, and pacifist inasmuch as it condemned the killing in the wars in which Europeans were indulging themselves.

With the swing in power away from church to state toleration became less a matter of one religious group tolerating another and more a matter of the independence of the individual from the demands of the state. Toleration is a relaxation of the demand for total conformity. It is therefore most endangered in a totalitarian age when spiritual or material wellbeing are believed to depend on uniformity and deviations are feared. The obverse of toleration is discipline *à outrance*. Medieval churchmen such as St Augustine, who feared for the survival of mainstream Christianity against heretics, and ideologues who fear for the survival of civilisation against communism, are – provided their premises be conceded – logically opposed to the toleration of personal idiosyncracies.

Authority in the Middle Ages was, in theory, shared between the religious and the lay power. In practice disputes between the two led to conflicts in which, for a while, the church triumphed but which ended in victory for the lay power, not however in the shape of the empire but of the smaller, more manageable state. Renaissance kings and princes retained enough of the flavour of the Middle Ages to dictate to their subjects what religion they should follow but found they were confronted by, and had to make concessions to, dissidents. Princes gradually abandoned their claim to enforce uniformity of religion because they were (with rare exceptions) less interested in beliefs than in power and money: they were satisfied so long as they might insist without challenge on strict obedience in civilian affairs, particularly the payment of taxes and military service.

Anti-establishment groups were primarily religious but from as early as the Renaissance they espoused other notions such as a better deal for women, anti-capitalism and egalitarianism; and a number of them were pacifist, for it is the essence of toleration to regard peace as more important than being right. But by no means all dissidents felt this. Luther sanctioned war. Calvin was as keen a disciplinarian as St Augustine. These Protestant champions wanted to transform the church-state relationship but not to dilute the claims of authority over the individual conscience. The spirit of compromise was to be found in the old churches as well as the new but its growth was slow since ecclesiastical debates were usually treated as occasions for proving the other side to be wrong. Peace on this basis depended on an identity of beliefs which was not attainable. But by the seventeenth century the violence of the clashes between (in particular) Roman Catholics and Calvinists caused a revulsion against dogmatic obduracy. Personal piety in religion and middle parties in politics found more favour. Although bigotry persisted and was transplanted into the New World (to Massachusetts, for example), toleration captured more minds: Lucius Cary, Viscount Falkland, was approvingly described as a bigot for toleration; the American colony of Maryland was established by Lord Baltimore, a Roman Catholic convert, on the basis of complete tolerance and with a population equally divided between Roman Catholics and Protestants; the founder of Rhode Island, Roger Williams, waged a war of words against the intolerance of Massachusetts.

Attempts to extend toleration to the military obligations of the individual to the state have been very largely an Anglo-Saxon phenomenon with some difference in emphasis between the United States, where their main basis has been religious, and Great Britain, where it has been freedom of conscience. In most of Europe a refusal to give military service has remained mutiny or treason up to and including the present century, although Denmark, the Netherlands and Switzerland accorded some relief in the Second World War. In the Soviet Union the rights of conscientious objectors were abolished in 1939. Canada exempted all Mennonites and Dukhobors on the grounds that they or their forbears went to Canada on those terms, although beyond these communities exception was granted in Canada only to adherents of a religion which forbade military service and only from combatant service.★

During the American Civil War a limited exemption was granted to members of religious bodies who, if drafted, became entitled to opt for non-combatant service. This scheme was applied again when the United States entered the First World War in 1917. The statute of that year which required men of 21–30 to register for service re-enacted the exemption for members of pacifist sects and a consequent Executive Order defined those branches of the army to which a conscientious objector might be directed. Although this Order referred to 'religious or other scruples', the American scheme was essentially designed to allow attested religious followers to slip through the net of conscription. Applicants had their genuineness examined by a board and, if successful, were drafted into agricultural (exceptionally industrial) jobs on a private's pay. Numbers were small: fewer than 65,000 applied on registration to be assigned to non-combatant service, which was conceded to the great majority of them. Recalcitrants included 142 who were sentenced to life imprisonment and a larger number who were given long sentences but all were released by the end of 1920, their offence being deemed to be expunged by the termination of the emergency. In the Second World War, as in the First, conscientious objectors were only a fraction of one per cent of those called up. In the Second the Selective Training and Service Act 1940 broadly followed the pattern set in the First. Roman Catholics overwhelmingly regarded the war as just while substantial majorities of Quakers and Mennonites also served. There was never any question that the right to conscientious abstention might impair the war effort.

In Great Britain, with its entrenched antagonism to compulsory military service, universal conscription was not introduced in the First World War until midway through 1916. The Prime Minister, H. H. Asquith, resisted for as long as he could in order that time and events might muster

★ Mennonites have also been granted special treatment in other countries. In the United States they were not obliged to wear uniform. In Russia they were allowed to choose hospital or other civilian work. In Germany they were conscripted into the army but allowed to do non-military work.

a sure majority in favour of conscription in cabinet, parliament and the country; in the event he lost only one member of his cabinet (John Simon). But by the winter of 1915–16 compulsory service had become inevitable if the western fronts were to be adequately manned. An attempt to boost volunteering (the Derby Scheme) showed in the autumn of 1915 that there were no longer enough volunteers and in January 1916 a first Military Service Act called up all unmarried men of 18–41. This was followed in May by universal male conscription which by the end of the war reached the 56-year olds. Certain categories of men engaged in work of national importance were excluded from the call up. Conscientious objectors, although not excluded, might be exempted from military service after call-up. Exemption was in practice mainly obtainable on religious grounds because the local tribunals created to administer this section of the Act could recognise a religious rule but were much less disposed to admit the sincerity of an individual's personal conscientious conviction. Exemption took various forms from the absolute to the qualified; those who sought and were granted qualified exemption became in effect soldiers without weapons, members of the services but behind the lines.

These dispensations aroused little public protest but their implementation somewhat more. Conscientious objectors had to appear before tribunals which were administered by the War Office, were staffed by people of conservative or blimpish instincts, were given muddled directions, were careless of the rules of evidence, applied different criteria in different parts of the country, acted like recruiting offices, and frequently displayed a disgusting insensitivity to the persons before them and a profound hostility to the legislation which they were supposed to apply. An applicant whose plea was rejected was handed over to the army and if he then refused to obey orders he became guilty of mutiny and liable to the death penalty. The military authorities played cat and mouse with these unwelcome and despised men, partly because the law left them with no alternative to a string of charges, court martials and prison terms. Thirty-four were at one time in danger of execution, although no death sentence was in fact carried out. Public opinion and the press regarded conscientious objectors as pro-German vermin who should never have been given the right to pit their private consciences against the needs of the nation. Nearly 6000 men refused on principle to appear before tribunals or to obey their rulings and were therefore consigned to the army and treated as deliquents until a way was found of getting most of them out of military prisons and into useful work. Another 9000 claimed absolute exception or qualified service. Four out of five were given exemption of some degree, 1700 absolutely.

In Great Britain resistance to military service was less specifically religious than in the United States. The No Conscription Fellowship, which was created soon after the outbreak of war and achieved 10,000 members mainly through advertising in newspapers, based its case on the dictates of the individual conscience rather than religious command: it denied the right of government to command personal service. Its leaders were on the whole unreligious. The Fellowship of Reconciliation on the other hand, founded about the same time, was mainly organised by the non-established churches and betokened a survival of Christian pacifism. The Quakers, the most visible anti-war group, reaffirmed as a body their total oppostion to war but a third of the men of military age gave military service and most of the conscientious objectors among them chose alternative service rather than absolute exemption. Small sects – Plymouth Brethen, Christadelphians, Seventh Day Adventists, Jehovah's Witnesses and others – were more rigorously pacifist. The Anglican and Roman Catholic churches produced only small pacifist minorities. Non-religious objectors – moralists opposed to the evil of killing, intellectuals revolted by the stupidity of war, political activists who denounced the war as a bosses' ramp – were also few.

In the Second World War the business of adjudicating claims to exemption was handled by a Ministry of Labour and National Service and not by the War Office. A total refusal to serve in any capacity was again recognised and again unpopular, particularly if the grounds were socialist rather than religious. The objector had to be opposed to all war without discrimination, so that he was not an objector within the meaning of the Act if he applied his mind to the circumstances of the war in question. Qualified objectors were again much more numerous than absolutists and were given civilian work which was of value to the nation but did not require combat duty. Most of this work was on the land although in some areas conscientious objectors were not wanted either because they were disliked or because there was no shortage of agricultural labour. Fire fighting in the cities attracted some of the more courageous pacifists, and after the passing of the National Service Act 1941 conscientious objectors could be drafted into civil defence. Non-combatant service with the armed forces was regulated by the creation in 1940 of a Non-Combatant Corps. Everything was tidier than in the first war and there were more non-lethal services to perform owing to the war's wider range. One per cent of those conscripted professed conscientious objections, a slightly higher proportion than in the first war. There was less persecution inside and outside the armed forces, and although over a thousand recalcitrants were court-martialled the military authorities were wary of the heavy-handedness that had characterised an earlier generation. The temper of the times had changed.

Nevertheless the conscientious objector who stood by his convictions had a difficult time, mitigated though it might be by the strength of those convictions. These were not all pacifist. In the first war Richard Garnett objected to abandoning his personal responsibility for his own actions and so to promising blind obedience to anybody. Such broad attitudes attracted less sympathy than the simple refusal to kill, even though the sacredness of life was at the bottom of them. Objectors had to accept, in the words of one of them (B. N. Langdon-Davies), a 'clean sweep of all one's friends except the very few' and 'association with people who were in deadly earnest, angry and plunged in gloom'. To this loneliness and censure were added the threats, real and imagined, from the police. The treasurer of the No Conscription Fellowship kept all his papers at a friend's house; took no money from foreigners; and collected funds secretly and in one pound notes. This was the atmosphere of a conspiracy against the state in a Conradian novel and it did not end with the war. Conscientious objectors were victimised within the civil service for a decade and some employers refused to hire them. The state had recognised the conscientious objector's right but society widely, and sometimes nastily, did not.

Nor was the individual's choice whether to exercise his right an easy one. In the second war the pacifist might claim, as Clive Bell said in April 1941: 'If Hitler proposes peace this autumn I am all for accepting. . . . I am quite sure, whatever happens, war will never make the world a pleasanter place to live in.' Or he might, like Alix Strachey two months earlier, say: 'Hitlerism is worse than war.' A year earlier, in April 1940, Hester Chapman wrote: 'A nazi regime, concentration camps etc. are worse than death.' To which Ralph Partridge replied: 'Yes, but worse than whose death? Your young men friends? If not, suicide is the correct answer.' Clive Bell put peace first, Alix Strachey did not. To Hester Chapman who posed a value judgement Ralph Partridge replied that if life presented so frightful a dilemma the right thing to do was abandon life. Faced with present facts pacifists do not agree with one another. It is no discredit to them that they do not, for facts and values exist on different planes. Hitlerism threw this dilemma in the face of civilisation. Consider the question: What killed six million Jews, Hitlerism or the war? Either answer is in one sense correct.

III

In the breathing space between the two great wars of the twentieth century peace movements recovered hesitantly from the shock of the first, some professedly Christians, others socialist or thereabouts, all overshadowed by League of Nations lobbies created to support the developed internationalism of the League. In Great Britain the No More War Movement (1921), successor to the No Conscription Fellowship, asserted that all war and all military service were wrong, to which it added political aims for a 'new social order'. The Labour Party passed anti-war and pro-disarmament resolutions and pinned faith on the mechanisms of the League. A Conference on Politics, Economics and Citizenship (COPEC) at Birmingham in 1924 created an organisation which was a damp squib. Attempts to needle the established church into outright opposition to war got no further than a declaration by the Lambeth Conference of 1930 that 'war as a method of settling international dispute is incompatible with the teaching of Our Lord Jesus Christ'; hardly a novel proposition. The rise of air power with its presage of the bombing of cities, the rise of fascism and the abdications of the League (in Manchuria, in Ethiopia) gave the 1930s a more desperate flavour than the first postwar decade. In 1932 Dr. Maude Royden produced a scheme for a Peace Army to be inserted between combatants – a dotty idea in the context of the times but a remote forbear of Greenpeace and other post-World War II interventionist protesters. The Oxford Union's over-publicised resolution in February 1933 against fighting for king and country was variously interpreted as a tilt against crude nationalism or a vote in favour of the Covenant of the League and disarmament. Later in that year a surprising Conservative defeat in a by-election in London's East Fulham, was an admonition to the government to take the League and the current disarmament conference more seriously. But most characteristic of these trends were two disparate expressions of popular opinion: the Peace Ballot of 1934, which epitomized the hopes invested in the League and disarmament, and the Peace Pledge Union, which was created in 1936 as a bid to affect the course of events by popular action.

The British Peace Ballot was sparked off by an obscure local initiative at Ilford in Essex where a group of people circulated a questionnaire at the beginning of 1934. This venture led to a national inquiry which, at a cost of £12,000, elicited over 11 million replies to five questions about the League and disarmament. The questions, with the percentage of affirmative votes, were: Are you in favour of the League of Nations (96)? Are you in favour of an all-round reduction in the level of armaments by international agreement (91)? Are you in favour of all-round abolition of national military and naval aircraft by international agreement (83)? Do you consider that the manufacture and sale of armaments for private profit should be prohibited by international agreement (91)? Finally, a double-barrelled question: Should other nations combine to stop an attack by (a) economic and non-military measures or, if necessary, military measures (87,59)? Not every respondent answered all the questions. The last question, which clearly caused the most heart-searching, elicited 6.5 million yeses and 2.26 million noes, but to all other questions the yeses ranged between 84 and 95 per cent of the votes cast on that question. This eccentric exercise in democracy was much ridiculed but nevertheless provided unexpectedly powerful evidence of what a substantial slice of the people wanted to see done. It did not give any clues to what these same people would do if their wishes were not followed: it was an expression of opinion, not a promise of action. The respondents, by huge majorities otherwise familiar only in dictatorships, wanted the League to work and the government to work it; they wanted mutual disarmament and controls over the arms industry. The ballot gave no indication of popular views about unilateral disarmament which figured neither in the questionnaire nor in general debate. The framers of the ballot certainly, and the respondents presumably, believed that disarmament must be international or not at all. There was less support for specific action on military aircraft whose abolition the respondents either did not much want or believe in. As a measure of the level of pacifism the ballot is indecisive although those who answered yes to question 5(b) were definitely not pacifists (as distinct from peace lovers), while those who answered yes to question 1 might be said to be non-pacifist by implication since the Covenant of the League envisaged the use of military force. The ballot contained no question to force upon the respondent the paradox of making war in the interests of peace.

The beginnings of the Peace Pledge Union were as unpretentious as those of the Peace Ballot in Ilford. Canon H. R. L. (Dick) Sheppard of St. Martin-in-the-Fields, London, issued in October 1934 a letter asking for written and signed personal refusals to support war. The response was not at first great but it was enough to encourage Sheppard to persist, to attract 7000 people to a meeting in the Albert Hall in July 1935 and to create the next year the Peace Pledge Union with 800 local branches, a paper, *Peace News*, a programme of public meetings, and eventually 136,000 members. Although essentially pacifist the Union attracted the attention and support of people, young and old, who were distressed about such things as unemployment and the Spanish Civil War and were generally distrustful of government. The Union was predominantly left wing and sometimes aggressively so in spite of its middle-to-upper-class complexion. It was caught in the classic dilemma: Can pacifism stop a war? In the context of the nation as a whole its membership was exiguous and in the end impotent. It issued a call to which far too few responded partly because they thought that Hitler ought to be stopped and could only be stopped by war, and partly on the wider grounds that a popular movement is to be weighed by its effectiveness and that pacifism lacked clout. If and so far as people asked themselves how they might stop a war, they probably thought it would be better to murder Hitler than to promise not to fight him or demonstrate against him in the streets of British cities. When war came in 1939 the Peace Pledge Union faded sadly and naturally away.

The ineffectiveness of pacifist and cognate movements in the interwar years was not merely a vote of practical no-confidence. These movements failed too to win the moral argument. The optimistic determination of the twenties to prevent a second World War through international organisation and co-operation was undermined in the thirties not only by disillusion with the League but also by the reintroduction of an abiding moral issue. The internationalists who supported the Covenant of the League assumed that keeping the peace ranked above everything else. So too did most pacifists. But the rise of Hitler threw doubt on this proposition and persuaded millions of people that war was not the ultimate evil. Bertrand Russell, who abandoned the pacifism of a lifetime in 1940, was only a particularly eminent example of the impact of Hitler's barbarity on people who, although in little danger of falling victim to it personally, were so repelled that they felt it right and necessary to fight it. War moved up the order of moral priorities. Whether this assessment can or should still prevail in the nuclear age is one of that age's main questions – as is the question whether revulsion against acceptable ideas should engender the same aggressive instincts as revulsion against unacceptable actions. In the thirties many people were keener to undo nazi Germany than to avoid war, and so they got war – which may have been right and just. If in the nineteen-eighties people are keener to undo the Soviet Union than to avoid (nuclear) war, they may again get war believing it to be right and just. This is not to say that they relish war in a militaristic spirit, only that they may approve it to the point of willing it.

6

The power of example

An argument or assertion can be rendered many times more potent by the spells woven about it by an exceptional individual. The personal voice and the lone example have a specially telling, moving and memorable power. Among the individual champions of peace are two principal prototypes: the man who refuses to go to war because it is wicked and he who refuses because it is senseless. The one is guided by his conscience which lays him under orders superior to military command, while the other is compelled by reason to an imperious disdain. The present century provides examples of both types in the pious peasant Franz Jäggerstätter, martyred for his stubbornness, and the arrogant intellectual G. F. Nikolai, exiled by his. Two far more famous figures – L. N. Tolstoy, at once moralist and intellectual, and M. K. Gandhi, moralist and idiosyncratic politician – also took a lonely stand against violence and war and suffered for it. What these men did is striking. What they achieved is harder to assess.

Franz Jäggerstätter (1907–43) was a loner whose fate would be merely pathetic if it were not also grandly tragic. He was an illegitimate peasant who, when his native Austria was seized by Hitler's Reich, alone in his village denounced nazism and who, when the Reich went to war, refused to serve it: he refused to pay his taxes or to obey the call-up. He was not a clever man, nor was he sophisticated or well educated. After a happy and even exuberant adolescence he experienced a religious illumination whereafter he was oppressed by a strong sense of evil. His religious beliefs became obsessive and his observances immoderate but he did not plague others with them and he was not in any commonly accepted sense deranged. His peculiarity lay in the inflexibility of his beliefs. He was convinced that the nazis were bad men and, above all, enemies of religion, and he was disgusted by the failure of Austrian Roman Catholics to speak out against Hitler. He particularly blamed the priesthood for betraying its charge. He made no secret nor any great parade of his views. He was deaf to family and friends who tried to get him to bend with the times and save his skin. He neither sought martyrdom nor gloried in its prospect but was utterly unable to do otherwise than he did. He was not an unqualified pacifist but was resolved to have no part in nazi wars, maintaining that the evil of the nazis would unerringly be reflected in the wars they waged – the obverse of the holy war which is just because it is divinely ordained. His position was logical. Yet everybody, including the authorities who eventually took him prisoner, tried to turn him away from his refusal to compromise while even his church refused to applaud him until his death caused him to be talked of as a saint. There could be no more striking example of the loneliness of the good man who will make no pact with evil nor find ways to judge it to be not as bad as all that. He did not believe that black clouds have silver linings and was not prepared to pretend that they do. So in the end he was hauled off to Berlin, condemned to death for treason and executed in August 1943. He was 36.

Jäggerstätter's life and death command attention because they are abnormal, admiration because they are courageous. At the same time they offend because they shame. Most people believe that Jäggerstätter and his like are right in what they believe and in what they do: they are morally superior. Nevertheless most people will not follow their example. Even Jesus, apparently a far more charismatic figure than Jäggerstätter, had only a small following in his lifetime and for many generations thereafter, and has been more honoured than emulated. The majority lacks faith and courage of such intensity as Jäggerstätter's and will concede to him approbation without imitation: to invert a famous saying, *non morituri te salutamus:* we salute you but have no wish to die. Over against Franz Jäggerstätter, the peasant loner, stands G. F. Nikolai, the intellectual loner. Both were

men of stubborn conviction but whereas the one was forced
into recalcitrance by his conscience telling him not to fight
in a wicked war the other was no less powerfully swayed
by war's futility. Nikolai (1874–1964) was a German heart
specialist, polymath and pacifist who wrote against war
during a war, as Aristophanes did – a severely impressive
analysis but no easy read, entitled *The Biology of War*. He is
remembered, however, not by his book but by his actions.
He revolted with aristocratic and arrogant indignation
against the stupidity of war, arguing – against the social
Darwinians – that war, so far from nurturing the survival
of the fittest race, would destroy the whole of European
civilisation and even the entire human species. He therefore
denounced national patriotism and, when called up into the
army by war, got much sport by taunting superior officers
who were his intellectual inferiors. After *The Biology of War*
was published in Switzerland in 1915 he fled from Germany
to Denmark. When the war ended he hoped for a social
revolution in Germany but found the socialist regime of Fritz
Ebert to be no more than the old system with a new face.*
Post-1919 Germany was not a comfortable place for rationalist intellectuals, particularly spiky ones like Nikolai, and
colleagues and students combined to drive him out of his
university post. In 1922, hounded as a wartime anti-German,
his life perhaps in danger, he abandoned Germany for South
America and spent the second half of his ninety years in
Argentina (1922–36) and Chile (1936–64). In his public life
he was a fighter, in his private life so egocentric as to be
almost a monster. His courage, which was indubitable,
particularly during the war, came largely from disdain for
his fellows, his pacifism from a logic as implacable as Jäggerstätter's although of a very different stamp. His example,
again like Jäggerstätter's has been more admirable than
productive and, for all the high eccentricity of their lives,
the names of both men are now barely known. Each has his

* He had some sympathy with the Spartacists on the left of the socialist
spectrum but was hostile to their methods and to their enthusiasm for
Lenin. He had neither political ambitions for himself nor party ties but
engaged in a good deal of speaking and pamphleteering on pacifism and
on international problems from a standpoint akin to Woodrow Wilson's
liberalism.

biographer: *In Solitary Witness: The Life and Death of Franz Jäggerstätter* by Gordon Zahn (1964) and *The Nikolai Case* by W. Zuelzer (1982). These two books are memorials to forgotten men whose convictions and values defy their personal oblivion.

II

Count Lev Nikolaevich Tolstoy (1828–1910) on the other hand was world famous in his lifetime and has remained so ever since. In the last part of his life, his place in European literature assured, Tolstoy turned to making the world a better place. He too was a figure apart but he neither withdrew into himself nor to a far-away land, for he was a natural teacher and publicist as well as a loner – one of his many contradictions. He was never a private man. He preached the virtues of simplicity and the do-it-yourself life, living without servants, although originally endowed with the means to have many. In his early days he started and himself taught in a school on his estates at Yasnaya Polnya and as he grew older his life was increasingly given over to teaching at large through books (his last novel *Resurrection* is among other things a moral tract), pamphlets, talk and example. His main theme was peace.

Tolstoy was a man of broad culture, a conscious participant in a European civilisation whose most vigorous manifestations in his lifetime were the mixed brew of Enlightenment rationalism and post-Enlightenment romanticism. Brought up in this (essentially western European) intellectual and emotional environment he was also a Russian, intensely absorbed in the Russian past and concerned about the Russian present; and he was no less profoundly a Christian. As a Russian his Christianity played a different role in his make-up than the Christianity of a western artist or thinker. The main stream of European civilization has flowed from Greece and Rome with a Christian tributary, but in the Russian variant these roles have been reversed: the great classical educators of the west from Socrates to Cicero have been less pervasive in Russia where the Greco-Roman inheritance, received through and diluted by Byzantium, has been dominated by Christianity and not the other way round.*

Tolstoy's preoccupation with peace was both in-born and nurtured by current events, not a sudden conversion but – from the 1870s onward – a gradually accentuated shift in emphasis as he felt driven to abandon literature for action because he judged action to be something superior which he ought not to shirk. The basis for this shift was religious but his religion brought him more perplexity than comfort as he laboured to reconcile his interpretation of the Christian gospel with the attitudes of the Russian Orthodox church on the one hand and with his rationalist heritage on the other.† When still quite young he set himself the task of founding a new religion but he lacked the single-mindedness with which the founders of religions override the intrusions of reason. He had a natural bent towards religion but it was impeded by his powerful intellect which blocked the traditional path to faith by an act of will, so that in spite of much striving (the Carlylean verb imposes itself) he failed to construct a faith capable of leading him into calm waters or his followers to a coherent programme. He has been likened to an Old Testament prophet but the comparison is inept on two counts: he lacked the certainties of the prophets and his real refuge was not the Old but the New Testament. He came to believe that the core of a true faith is to be found in the Sermon on the Mount which he revered as the inspired utterance of a great, good, non-divine man and from which

* For a brilliant analysis of the tangle of contradictions which both made and unmade Tolstoy see Isaiah Berlin's *The Hedgehog and the Fox*.
† He is in this matter akin to Plato, also a religious man with a firm belief in a divinely created and ordered world. Like Tolstoy, Plato was fascinated by a religion which he could not fully embrace (in his case Orphism) and was also a superlative practitioner in the use of words, images and myths.

he derived five negative injunctions: to abjure anger, adultery, the swearing of oaths (to authority), patriotism and war.

Like many moralists before him Tolstoy regressed, painfully and against the content of his early upbringing, to early Christianity. He managed to persuade himself that a new world was about to dawn. He scorned and castigated meliorists and liberals who occupied themselves with schemes for making the world better by what, for him, was tinkering with ephemerals. This convenient notion of the imminent end of a bad world and the arrival of a better one enabled him to brush aside or overlook a number of problems rooted in the-way-things-are. He both shared the early Christian distrust of the state and contrived to dismiss it; he anticipated those extremists who argue that the coercive state is intrinsically a form of violence which justifies their counter-violence. He himself lived in an authoritarian state stained with tyranny, gross injustice and – for part of his life – serfdom, but he did not regard democracy as a cure for these ills since western Europe's democratic systems struck him as no more than a modest deconcentration of the power of an equally modestly expanded elite. He opposed civil as well as military service to the state (for example, jury service) on the grounds that the state was a conspiracy sustained by force, propaganda and bribes. He hated the state as the seat of authority, the maker of wars and – with private property – the source of violence.

Tolstoy's piercing diagnosis tempted him, however, into an unfounded conclusion. He asserted – and this fundamental assertion is false – that there is an alternative to force as a basis for society. Furthermore he had no use for schemes for an international order based on the state and regarded such schemes as cloaks for the preservation of the state. Neither states nor a league of states would prevent wars. The only way to stop a war was a mass refusal to fight it.

Tolstoy formed and proclaimed these views with a total disregard for politics and political realities which made his assertions as naive as they were vigorous. Yet he was no armchair spinner of generalizations but was moved as much by current events as by moral propositions. His *Confession* (1879), which is the first in the canon of his politico-moral writings, was composed in the aftermath of the frightful cruelties of the Russo-Turkish war of 1877–78 which helped to turn his ideas into obsessions, devote the rest of his life to anti-war campaigns, castigate his church for feebleness and backsliding (it excommunicated him in 1901), develop his belief that evil must be combated not with a sword but with love, and confirm his condemnation of flesh-eating and corporal punishment. He was also much stirred by the persecution of the Dukhobors or, as they were called in Russia from the eighteenth century, Molokans. The Dukhobors were simple Christians who objected to wars and bearing arms and had been confined by Nicholas I to the Caucasus, in which wild area their prejudice against arms was relaxed and no call to military service reached them until the end of the century. When it did it split them. Peter Verigin, who read Tolstoy's writings, revived their pristine beliefs and practices (and added vegetarianism, teetotalism and chastity) and embarked in 1895 on a three-year battle with the Russian state which took him to gaol, to Siberia and eventually – with financial help from Tolstoy – to North America. He took 7,500 Dukhobors with him, about half the Russian community, and refused in 1906 a Russian invitation to return. In Canada new splits occurred and the more rigorous groups resorted to nudity (they were perhaps the first streakers) and arson to advertise their views. In Russia most of the remaining Molokans gave combatant service in the First World War.

Tolstoy was not a systematic thinker. His later writings and teaching are less enduring and less effective testimony against war than *War and Peace* and his stories. *War and Peace* is a huge manifesto against war but it makes its points not dialectically but in vignettes, by its unsurpassed visual impact and its delineation of fictional characters, by artistry rather than argument.

For all his vehemence he had something of the innocence of early romantic poets, an innocence which presents scenes and people as lone, small objects in a vastly wonderful world. But his world slides into unreality and his prescriptions strain credulity. His hatred of violence was so complete that he said that he would not lift a finger to shield women and children or impede the madman or drunkard. He disapproved of famine relief, describing famine as a consequence of sin and relief as vomit sicked up by the rich; yet in a crisis in 1891–93 he engaged vigorously in relieving the needy. He condemned the seclusion of lunatics as an easy option which brushed the affront under the carpet and so eroded the need and the will to change the system which itself produced lunatics (and criminals). He argued, again with a lack of common sense, that it is better to run the risk that women and children may be killed. Loathing violence, he imposed on himself the rule of never responding with violence to violence and pointed out that if everybody did likewise there would be an end to violence and to war. This is good logic but poor sense, since it is inconceivable that everybody will do likewise. His letter to Alexander III urging on that monarch forgiveness for the assassins of his father is a marvellously moving appeal to a man in a high place to set an example and so change the ways of the world: it was unsuccessful.

Tolstoy's own life was full contradictions. His marriage was a disaster and he was indifferent to all but one of his nine surviving children. He asserted the compatibility of marriage and chastity. He disapproved of private property but gave his own not to his peasants but to his children. A great artist, he was unsure of the purpose and status of art; he did not, like Chernyshevsky (and later the Stalinists), maintain that art is ancillary to moral and social aims but he did at times appear to disapprove of art which was accessible only to a class or elite. He accepted that man has an instinctive feeling that it is praiseworthy to smite the devil; he went on to argue that it were better for man to be cured of this propensity, and that he may be; but he fails to show how the devil may be and so seems content to give the victory to the devil. Non-resistance to evil entails the triumph of evil.

Tolstoy approached the special and culminating evil of war from the angle of his hatred of the state, not simply the state as warmaker but the state in all its manifestations and demands. He does not believe in reforming or curbing the state. He was concerned with war throughout his life. His stories, from his first works to *Hadji Murad* at the very end, reflect his fascination with war. He saw war as a young man and wrote about what he saw in his Sebastopol Sketches. In *War and Peace* – whose eventual title he chose from Proudhon's non-fictional work, *La Guerre et la Paix* – war provides the background to his accounts of a family and its fortunes, a nation and its sufferings, the nature of history, and the responsibility of the individual in the course of great events. In describing the appalling suffering at Borodino (one of the most frightful massacres in human history) he convinces his readers that war, although it may be just, is also too horrible to be tolerated. Many years earlier, in a story called *The Raid*, he had already shown himself more concerned with what war does to the individual than with how or why it is fought; he was, in his own words, more interested to discover with what feelings a soldier kills another than how the armies were arranged at Austerlitz or Borodino.

Tolstoy can make his readers sicken at the thought of war. But it was not the whole of his life's purpose, for he wanted to get war, if not abolished, at least much curtailed. He was right when he pointed to the state as the chief repository of power and an organisation not to be trusted with it, although many of his contemporaries did not go so far as to maintain that the state could never be an instrument for good. Socialists, hoping to place the government of the state in peaceful socialist hands, thought otherwise, but Tolstoy's prejudices and his Russian environment told him that the state and its government are the playthings of small groups of powerful and selfish men constantly playing tricks on their fellow citizens to persuade them that what the minority want – including aggression and wars – its meritorious. This pessimistic theory of politics is an extension of Tolstoy's firsthand view of how wealthy landlords could and did manipulate those in their power for selfish and unjust ends. He treated the state as a grasping landlord writ large and was never persuaded that the state might be made amenable to better ends by the democratic institutions with which western Europe was experimenting. The state was therefore an engine unalterably programmed for tyranny and war.

But this conclusion led to a dead end and Tolstoy seems to have perceived the vanity of his conclusion. Although a domineering man, he was also fearful. He was very ready to tell people how to behave but his didactic urge was checked by the awe which warned him that he might after all not be right and so brought him to despair. Nobody is at once so certain and so uncertain as Tolstoy, and so at the end of his long life he adopted certain fixed absolutes as rafts to support his titanic nature. He had no allies or friends.

Great men come in different shapes. One of these is the Titan – creature of monumental impact, possessed of huge creative mastery, simultaneously driven by an unmastered moral quest, unquiet therefore and disquieting. Tolstoy was a Titan. So was Beethoven and it is no accident that their combined lifespan (1770–1910) covers a period in European history which begins in *Sturm und Drang* and proceeds through the turbulence of romanticism, religious doubt and moral relativism: Beethoven's Heiligenstadt Testament and Tolstoy's Confession are two of the key documents of this period.

The Titan's illumine great issues in flashes which the more ordinary mortal finds both awe-inspiring and difficult to appreciate. They stir and perplex; they do not resolve. Tolstoy in *War and Peace*, *Anna Karenina*, *The Kingdom of God is within you* and many stories and pamphlets – like Beethoven in his last quartets, ninth symphony and elsewhere – commands attention to things that matter greatly: happiness, truth, peace. But he does not make them easy to grasp and he settles nothing. His battles are with himself: he is his own chief adversary. Tolstoy matters for his protest, not for his prescription. He proclaimed, with the power of his personality and his fame, that violence and war are wrong but he had no cure for them. The moralist sees what is wrong but is not the person to put it right: his function is to mould attitudes, not to draft plans or constitutions.

III

Tolstoy conducted a voluminous correspondence with admirers all over the world, including, towards the end of his life, with Mohandas Karamchand Gandhi in South Africa. Gandhi abhorred violence as heartily as Tolstoy but, unlike Tolstoy, he was an alert politican whose high principles were yoked to tactical cunning. He developed by personal example and grit his belief that political ends can be won by non-violent action, including civil disobedience to the law. His main aims, which he failed to achieve, were the liberation of a (united) India from British rule without bloodshed and the fashioning of an Indian way of life based on traditional rural crafts and minimal decentralized authority. The end of the British raj was in fact precipitated by events other than Gandhi's campaign (notably the Second World War and the continuing erosion of the British will to stay); liberation was accompanied by terrible killings and partition; and Gandhi's romantic village socialism has been treated as a romantic idiosyncracy. Nevertheless Gandhi scored over the years a number of striking successes which made him perhaps the most famous man in the world – even more famous, one must suppose, than Tolstoy – and created an enduring legend. At the centre of the legend is the frail but resolute figure of Gandhi himself as the apostle of non-violence. Because of what he set out to achieve his name has never been far from civil rights and pacifist movements of the later twentieth century.

M. K. Gandhi (1869–1948) was a younger son in a family with an hereditary claim to superior political office in the small western Indian state of Porbandar. He trained as a lawyer and then departed not only from his state but from India. His reasons for this emigration, which was a ritual offence, were negative. He was unhappy at home and so at the age of 24 accepted a job in Natal. There he stumbled into politics but, once in, hardly ever stumbled again. He was quick witted, intellectually something of a magpie, nimble on his political feet and prepared to make tactical compromises or retreats. He was influenced by Ruskin, Thoreau and Tolstoy as well as by his Indian background and was attracted by religions (in the plural), including spiritual offshoots like theosophy. Never a totally or exclusively convinced adherent of any one faith he was an eclectic who owed some of the veneration bestowed on him in later life to his seeming ability to take and reconcile the best from many beliefs without rancour or meanness. The rebellious-ness in his character and its strength came from obstinacy and courage rather than a Tolstoyan rage.

Gandhi's apprenticeship to politics was uncommonly long, even in a long life. He spent 21 years in South Africa where there were about 100,000 Indians. This numerically insig-nificant community was given political prominence by the government's attempts to throttle its civil rights by a Fran-chise Amendment Act and, later, an Asiatic Relations Act. Gandhi organised non-violent opposition to these measures and paid his first visit to London in connection with the latter. His standing was further advanced by his involvement as a lawyer in a case concerning the validity of non-Christian marriages and then once more on the broad political front by his opposition to the Immigration Restriction Act. He organised peaceful demonstrations with the object of swamping the prisons with people normally considered to be inoffensive and law-abiding. He had become a political leader with a distinctive style whose main purpose was to embarrass, shame or ridicule the authorities where he could not coerce them. At the same time he kept contact with them, making himself an acknowledged interlocutor who preferred dialogue to confrontation and was willing to accept partial success: he succeeded on marriages but failed on immigration.

Gandhi left South Africa in 1914, was in London when war began and returned in January 1915 to an India which knew little about him. His career in South Africa had made him a successful lawyer and taught him a good deal about the professions of journalist, pamphleteer and politician. He had become hooked on helping the helpless and accustomed to dealing with people in high places. He returned to India as a reformer as well as a nationalist.

He was ambivalent about the British but firmly opposed to their rule over Indians. He was not an absolute pacifist. On both these issues – the political and the moral – his qualified positions were an asset in that they extended his freedom of manoeuvre and his credibility. During the Boer War he had been actively pro-British (for him the underdogs were not the Boers but the Indians) but he was disgusted by British behaviour in the Zulu rebellion of 1906. He supported the British war effort in the First World War and up to a point in the Second, conscious in both cases of his legal obligations as a British subject and, in the Second, of the rightness of the British cause against nazi Germany. He encouraged recruiting for the armed forces and although personally predisposed towards non-combatant service treated the distinction between combatant and non-combatant service as secondary.

Gandhi's Indian heritage was mixed, with Hindu, Buddist and Jain strands. The Hindu gods and epics are as fearsome as any but the Bhagavad Gita – the song of Krishna which is enveloped in the immense Hindu epic Mohabharata – extols non-violence or *ahimsa* (literally, the negation of injury or harm). Buddhism is more clearly pacific.

Sidhartha Gautama, the Buddha, who lived in the sixth century BC (563–483), tried to rationalise existence. His activity was thinking. He mentions no god and there is nothing supernatural or extranatural in his system which became a religion (if it is one) only long after his death. Buddhist communities or *sanghas*, for which the Buddha formulated nearly 300 rules, did not practise a religion or teach a philosophy but they observed certain precepts, one of which forbade the taking of any kind of life. Buddhism offers also a social order in which the individual, both now and hereafter, is a subordinate particle in the cosmos. The Buddha was an extreme anti-individualist and, so far from retreating into a wilderness in order to safeguard the individuality, established his *sanghas* in or near towns. The *sangha*, which is a centre for meditation as practised by the Buddha himself, has the corporate duty of teaching behaviour by example and so extending Buddhism by peaceful permeation of society.

In the third century BC the emperor Asoka (ruled 269–237) made an uneasy attempt to fuse Buddhism with the monarchical state. Asoka inherited a vast Hindu empire based on war and expanded it, but years of bloodshed turned his mind to thoughts of peace (like Augustus after Actium he had had enough) and after flirting with various religions he was gradually converted to Buddhism and to diverting into social programmes the energies which he had expanded on war. His contemporary, Vardhamana Mahavira, effectively the founder of India's third main faith, Jainism, also preached the priority of social over military budgets. Asoka himself has remained for 2000 years one of the most striking figures in India's turbulent history as the great warrior turned to peaceful pursuits.

Gandhi did more than imbibe the teachings of India's gods, sages and heroes. He added something of his own which has been largely responsible for the flavour of the Gandhism which the world beyond India has tried to assimilate and put into effect. This something is *satyagraha*.

Satyagraha, which Gandhi elaborated during his years in South Africa, means going for truth: *sat* = truth, *agrah* = to grasp. It is both a technique and a principle. As a technique it is indebted to Thoreau's thoughts on civil disobedience.★ Gandhi taught that the way to *sat* is love and that love for others begins with the regeneration of the self by purging it of selfishness. There are Buddhist echoes here, for the

---

★ Henry David Thoreau (1817–62) was one of those who believe that all government is bad, but he did not believe that it can be dispensed with. So the less of it the better. His attacks on government in his own day and place were focussed on slavery and the (unjustifiable) war with Mexico, evils so great that they had to be publicly condemned and resisted. His protest was peaceful, for he was not the man to throw a brick through a window, let alone a grenade at a statesman. He refused, for six years, to pay the toll tax although he willingly paid the highway tax. He regarded the right to rebel as self-evident: 'All men recognize the right to revolution; that is, the right to refuse allegiance to, and to resist, the government, when its tyranny or its inefficiency are great and unendurable.' He is a case of withdrawal and response. He retreated into rural solitude but came back into circulation to make his mark – not unlike the Benedictines who secluded themselves for 500 years and then in the eleventh century began to send eminent figures back into the world to do something to improve it.

Buddha taught that man is naturally good but unable to control his violent appetites unless these are disciplined by love, the alternative to violence. For Buddhists and for Gandhi this antithesis between violence and love is a key to personal conduct and not, as for Tolstoy, a critique of the state. Gandhi was also convinced as a matter of principle that the use of violence vitiates the purpose of a campaign. He therefore insisted that a political campaign must eschew violence and he was encouraged, by Thoreau among others, to believe that non-violence was effective as well as imperative. His uncompromising opposition to violence is one of the things that sets Gandhi apart from most leaders of popular movements and invests him with a moral crown. He realised that if violence is to be prevented from seeping into a popular movement, two things are necessary: strict discipline and willingness to call a halt if things get out of hand. These he supplied and enforced, on occasion by putting his own life at risk by fasting in order to constrain the forces he had unleashed. As a middle way between violence and merely passive resistance *satyagraha*, after its application to India's social and political problems, was adapted in other parts of the world as a technique of universal value.

Non-violence as a political tool, as distinct from a moral precept, does not figure in the Indian tradition. Nothing like Gandhi's way of doing politics had been seen there before him. India was, however, familiar with the strike or *hartal*, whose purpose was to shame an adversary into giving way or at least feeling bad. Gandhi saw the strike as an instrument of persuasion and conversion (an unkind name for it would be moral blackmail) and he adapted it both to the politics of race in South Africa and the politics of power in India. It entangled and infuriated his adversaries who wanted to play the political game by more conventional means – confrontation leading to victory – and labelled Gandhi a hypocrite and a crank. Yet Gandhi, like a medieval jouster, was set on scoring points rather than victory in a kind of dialectic in which respect breeds respect, truth breeds truth, and the outcome is a peaceful outfacing and eventual outsmarting of the enemy.

In the first interwar decade the British in India were by turns provocative and conciliatory while the second decade was dominated by constitutional debate. Throughout this period Gandhi tussled with the Indian National Congress as well as the British raj. The Congress, founded in 1885, was the protagonist of anti-imperialism and its leaders regarded Gandhi with suspicion and resentment, only veiled when Gandhi's popular acclaim made it imprudent to do otherwise. The Congress had ceased to regard British rule as more benevolent than exploitative and saw no way of getting rid of it without violence, especially when the end of the First World War brought a hardening of British attitudes which confirmed Congress prejudices. The Rowlatt Act of 1919 perpetuated wartime emergency measures such as indefinite imprisonment. The imposition of martial law in the Punjab, leading to the fearful massacre in the Jalianwallah Bagh at Amritsar where 400 were killed and 1200 wounded, showed the hard face of British rule, and insult was added to injury when the House of Lords refused to censure the commanding general. Indian Muslims were perturbed by the harsh treatment of Turkey by the Treaty of Sèvres in 1920 and by the abolition of the caliphate (not, as it happened, by Great Britain but by Kemal Ataturk). Gandhi was slower than the bulk of the Congress to abandon his loyalty to the British Crown and and even as he gradually altered his position he retained his attachment to non-violence. That the Congress tagged along behind Gandhi in these years marked a considerable achievement for the man who had only recently returned to India, lacked the hereditary or intellectual claims to leadership which abounded in the upper and professional classes, and insisted on tactics so patently ill suited to the tumultuous times. But against these disabilities was his record for getting things done and for getting attention.

Gandhi had not been slow to go his own way while the war was still on. In 1917 he took up the cause of indigo planters in Bihar who were being cheated by British landlords. He did so by angering and disobeying local officials, by talking sensibly to higher officials, by threatening to make more trouble than the issue was worth to the British government and by accepting a great deal but not the whole of what he was demanding. He became a national figure but then chose to return to the *ashram* which he had created two years earlier at Ahmedabad (it was modelled on the

Tolstoyan Phoenix Farm in Essex which he visited in 1910, with the addition of Ruskinian weaving and spinning) and bided his time. He lent his support to striking mill workers on the dual condition that they would neither go back to work on a compromise nor resort to violence and when the situation became desperate went on hunger strike. This move turned the tables in favour of the strikers and led in time to the formation of the first Indian labour union. He repeated these tactics against public authorities over local taxation, securing another partial victory. His popular repute grew and he began to be regarded by the British as a dangerous man. His standing was now recognised by the Viceroy who invited him to a conference on recruitment for war service where he repeated his view that subjects of the crown owed unconditional service – without, that is to say, exacting pledges in return regarding home rule or independence after the war. He was not afraid to annoy other Indians who were as nationalistic as he but less legalistic.

After the unhappy start to the post war years the British switched to a more conciliatory mode. The Rowlatt Act was repealed; liberal changes were introduced in press censorship, promotion prospects for Indians and excise duties; the Simon Commission on constitutional reform was set up and the possibility of dominion status was allowed to enter the debate. On the other hand no Indian was a member of the Simon Commission; the salt tax was doubled; dominion status was suspect as a device for fending off independence; and the results of the Round Table conferences of 1930–31 on the future government of India were barren. Gandhi stuck to non-violence although violence was frequently round the corner – in Bombay, for example, during the visit of the Prince of Wales in 1921. Gandhi fasted to stem the Bombay riots and called off his civil disobedience at Bardoli (a refusal to pay land tax) when it provoked violence. He was arrested, pleaded guilty to sedition, was sent to goal for six years and served two. When he came out in 1924 he was quickly engaged in a 21-day fast for Hindu-Muslim amity in the face of growing communal discord and he renewed his Bardoli protest. His career was beginning to look like a rather point-less roundabout but at Bardoli he secured yet another of his partial successes when government agreed to abate steep tax increases.

Gandhi and other Congress leaders were at one in boycotting the investigations of the Simon Commission and the British Labour government's first proposals for a Round Table conference because the British refused to promise even dominion status in advance. Early in 1930 the Congress accepted the urgings of those leaders who were insisting on full independence. In the same year Gandhi turned to more congenial business by campaigning against the government's salt monopoly. He made a long march to Dandi where, in defiance of the law, he made and sold salt. He was again arrested. While he was in prison the Round table conference approved a new federal constitution for India with the assent of non-Congress Indian participants. Gandhi was released and persuaded by the Viceroy to attend a second Round Table conference. The salt regulations were relaxed and Gandhi dropped his campaign against them and went to London where he aligned himself with the demand for independence. This the newly installed (mainly) Conservative government refused and Gandhi returned to India, civil disobedience and once more to prison where he remained until 1933. In these years Gandhi's aims became more radical but his methods were unchanged. They won him some minor successes but were fruitless on major constitutional issues.

Gandhi did not see the Second World War as either necessary or just but he was reluctant to take advantage of Great Britain in its hour of distress. He thought the Jews in Germany should practise non-resistance and persisted in this view even when the extent of the holocaust became known. In India he organised no mass movement but approved individual illegal acts until the failure of the Cripps mission in 1942 instigated the Quit India movement. Although designed as massive civil disobedience, this movement engendered widespread violence. The Viceroy blamed the disorders on Gandhi who was horrified, fasted for 21 days and seriously damaged his health. He and other leaders were arrested and Gandhi was not again a free man until May 1944.

He emerged to play a part in the grand drama of the

departure of the British from India and the terrible tragedies of its concomitant partition. Gandhi abhorred the partition, which the Congress reluctantly endorsed. His last fast in Calcutta stemmed the killings but only temporarily. He was assassinated on January 1948 by a young Hindu who believed that non-violent protest was craven nonsense.

Gandhi's career is a study of abnormality. It showed that non-violent civil disobedience may be a useful addition to the political armoury in exceptional circumstances. This is a limited assessment and thousands of people have judged otherwise, concluding that Gandhi displayed not only the virtue of non-resistance to evil but also the effectiveness of non-violence in a conflict. Yet Gandhi's ends were not achieved without violence in spite of his own strenuous efforts to stop its use. His main aim moreover – the dissolution of British rule – was brought about by many things. The British had been saying for a hundred years that they intended to leave India, had taken some steps to that end, and were showing signs of wanting to take more. They were already dislodgeable. Nor can it be convincingly argued that Gandhi's campaigns, either by making life difficult for the British authorities or by shaming them, were decisive in accelerating independence. What did that was the war.

Gandhi was a high perseverator but not a notable achiever. His perseverance was admirable and inspiring but he would have been the last to describe the grisly scenes of 1947 as a success. He did not exult. He had the supreme virtue of being easily stirred to indignation in South Africa by racial intolerance and injustice, in India by poverty and injustice. He was a political animal with a strange view of politics which he treated as the conduct of communal or national affairs within the bounds of non-violence. This makes politics a branch of ethics which, unlike everybody else's politics, subordinates ends to means. This is a recipe for virtue but not, except in very unusual circumstances, for success. Yet Gandhi has been judged by the world a success and in large measure to be judged a success is to be a success.

No judgement on Gandhi's public performance can escape the fact that he was something a great deal more than a politician. He became a symbol. His career led millions to believe that big problems may be settled without violence, so that he has a lasting place in the history of ideas as well as in the history of India. He inspired people and many of them placed him in the ranks of those who are expected, dangerously, to work wonders. His example fired the imagination, but in the last analysis the measure of its relevance to public affairs lies in this: that when his career in India began the main conflict was between Indians and British but before it ended the main conflict was between Hindus and Muslims, and that he made a profound mark on the former but barely affected the latter.

7

The power of protest

Popular involvement in public affairs has produced (as already noted) a boost to national warmaking on the one hand but also a countervailing stream of anti-war lobbying on the other. This second current, that of protest, has been the weaker but it has on balance waxed more than it has waned, most notably in Europe.

Protest is rooted in human nature and sanctioned by democratic theory. History discloses a number of broad categories. One is the protest against power: against, for example, the tightening authority of the centralising state or the expanding state. The *frondes* of the nobles in seventeenth-century France were protests against the central power of the French monarchy; the risings in seventeenth- and-eighteenth century Russia led by Cossacks (Bolitnikov and Razin, Bulavin and Pugachev) were protests against the expanding power of the Muscovy Tsardom. Both were directed against the state in one or another of its more menacing aspects. A second kind of protest is economic: bread riots are a primitive example, superseded in industrialised states by the more sophisticated and orderly strike of organised labour. In some situations the food riot and the strike may be combined, as for instance in Poland in 1970. The strike is most often directed against employers rather than the state but in roughly the same period there emerged also a third kind of protest – political protest – which, if not a product of the democratic revolution, has come into its own with that revolution and is directed chiefly against governments.

The main instruments of popular force generated by the industrial and democratic revolutions are the trade union and the political party. Each has its peculiar and restricted aims: better pay and conditions of work in the one case, winning votes and influencing leaders in the other. Both pursue these aims mainly by talking and arguing in bargaining sessions or political meetings, or by written offshoots such as the pamphlet or sympathetic press coverage. In the industrial area the war of words is backed ultimately by the threat to stop working or, in extreme exasperation, to sabotage the industrial round by violence – which may be illegal or even criminal. In the political field democracy, besides fostering the political party, recognises also rights of free speech and assembly and the propriety of extra-parliamentary and extra-party activity stemming from these rights – activity which may entail breaches of the civil or criminal law.

The stock examples of successful protest in Great Britain are the abolition of the slave trade and winning votes for women. Both were single-issue campaigns and were kicking at rickety doors. They accelerated changes already in the wind, persuading governments to do sooner what they seemed certain to do one day. More recently, in the United States and after the incursion of television into public debate, the single-issue campaign against the war in Vietnam affected – or may plausibly be judged to have affected – the conduct of the war: limiting the bombing of Cambodia and the cities of Hanoi and Haiphong and then bringing the troups back home.

But if the effectiveness of popular protest is related to numbers, then the single-issue campaign has weakness as well as strength. Its concentration on a particular issue gives it the strength of clear, firm purpose but by the same token reduces the ambit of its popular appeal. The failure of most popular movements is that they are not popular enough: they are popular in the literal sense but in the colloquial sense unpopular. Disarmament movements, for example, are organised by 'ordinary' people but not enough people join them. There is, therefore, always a case for the more broadly based campaign which is an agglomeration of compatible causes notwithstanding the accompanying danger of fissiparous squabbling. Bracketing disarmament with, for example, anti-pollution or anti-vivisection does at least assemble a larger company whose members are very broadly like-minded.

In the nineteen-thirties the main issues were poverty and discrimination against the poor (the reduction, for example, in the real value of the dole given to the growing numbers of unemployed by the British state). Demonstrations such as the Jarrow March had middle-class sympathisers and organisers but the hunger marchers themselves came from the unemployed working class. By contrast, the typical protesters of the period after World War II were not the poor but the young, not the working class but the middle class. And although the Vietnam war and, more generally, nuclear weapons were prominent topics they were not the only ones. Protest was more broadly based and often therefore less pointed or less consistent. 'Ban the Bomb' was as good a slogan as 'Votes for Women' but a typical protest movement of the mid-century was less single-minded about the bomb than the suffragettes had been about the rights of women.

The special concern of youth is logically education and particularly, for the more thoughtful, university education. This the young of the postwar period have judged to be unsatisfactory and their attacks on it, sometimes a rumble and sometimes a bang, have been the ground for a passacaglia of protest movements in a number of countries. In West Germany, for example, universities were archaic in structure, their classes were overcrowded and their lectures frequently bad. The same was true elsewhere in Europe, a fact which created points of contact among the increasingly itinerant young of many countries. Although West German students had been granted votes in certain academic bodies, they had not bothered to make much use of them. This passive attitude changed, however, in tune with political change. During the fifties only one in three of young West Germans between the ages of 14 and 21 expressed interest in politics when questioned by opinion-seekers, but a survey carried out in 1965 showed that more than half of those in this age bracket had become politically minded. The more active of the politically alert young came from stable professional, official or self-employed families; more than nine out of ten lived with their parents; the better educated they were, the more involved they felt. Their reading was undented by television (which had reduced sales of thrillers only); they were keen followers of sports and more interested in music, theatre and dance than religion. They differed from their elders most obviously in their open espousal of sexual freedom but were little addicted to drugs and scorned the brawling and beer-swilling characteristics or earlier generations of Germans. The greater part of them were an uncomplicated lot with a strong vein of seriousness and their political activities sprang from this seriousness, but this new political alertness was turning to radicalism under the pressure of events.

The most obtrusive of these events was the war in Vietnam which gave on unexpected twist to the politics of youth in West Germany and elsewhere in Europe. West Germany was looking for a political issue. Postwar recovery had been succeeded by a duller phase and the Grand Coalition formed by the two main parties at the end of 1966 removed much of the sting from parliamentary and political debate, while also obfuscating the SPD's claim to a distinct and progressive role in the country. Although Vietnam was remote, reactions to the war there were uncomplicated and protest groups which did not find it easy to agree on domestic grievances or tactics could without difficulty agree that the war was evil and must be stopped. External issues, although normally less pressing, provided a better focus and rallying point than domestic ones.

Yet domestic issues are fitter for action, if only because the action has to be at home. European students do not imagine that their protests can change the policies of the United States but they may hope to affect authorities nearer home, whether in government or universities. In the mid-sixties the particularly vociferous Berlin students found in Rudi Dutschke – the chairman of the Berlin branch of the SDS (Sozialistischer Deutscher Studentenbund – a leader of commanding personality. Dutschke, a young man in his late twenties from a well educated Protestant Christian background, had no faith in parliamentary procedures, believed that justice was unobtainable without a fight and advocated militancy – oratorical, physical and literally incendiary. He became the star of the year of violence, 1968, when the radical minority in the student body became big enough to make a considerable splash and the German press gave daily reports under large headlines of battles between students and police and wrote worriedly and sometimes extravagantly of civil war. Besides their attacks on university authorities and other domestic concerns the students gave special prominence to American imperialism in South East Asia and, as disciples of Franz Fanon and Che Guevara, to the plight of the poor and oppressed all over the world.

In April 1968 Dutschke was shot and badly wounded by a youth of 23 and battles were fought for several days in several cities. As the demonstrators concerted their activities the authorities labelled them an organized conspiracy intent on the destruction of democracy under the control of Moscow. But they never had a chance of overturning the established order once the government, overcoming its initial preference for keeping aloof, licensed unbridled police intervention. The protestors were overcome. Old style workers' strikes supplanted student riots and in 1970 the SDS, fragmented, dissolved itself. Small changes were made in some universities. The Free University of Berlin, founded in 1948 with a degree of student participation, extended this participation in faculties and university government but radical students were hostile to reforms which they stigmatized as cosmetic; the post of President, extended from 2 years to 7, was won in 1969 by a 30-year-old professor of sociology by 61 votes to 49 in the Council of the University. But the world's poor and oppressed remained that way and the war in Vietnam was unaffected by these events in Europe. Similar commotions in France and elsewhere had almost precisely similar results.

For the protestors these were dispiriting, and those among them who were looking for results were surprisingly quickly reabsorbed into the large mass of the passively disgruntled. But those few who were moved by principle rather than expectations were not so easily snuffed out. They waited for time to leaven another lump. It came in 1980 with the triumph in the United States of Ronald Reagan as the chosen instrument of the rampant right and this time the protest was more clearly political and international.

II

The political protest of the mid-twentieth century was rooted in two things above all: the temper of the younger generations and the fear of nuclear war.

The young of this time were more than usually scornful and distrustful of their elders and particularly of the ruling class. This was not surprising in those countries – Germany and France above all – where the rulers and those who profited from their rule had brought disaster before and during World War II. Most of continental Europe experienced this upheaval but in most countries the ruling class escaped popular retribution either (in the west) by resurfacing in moderately chastened shape or (in the east) by being submerged by Soviet imperialism and its local instruments. The sense of grievance and humiliation of the younger generation was not vented. Even where the war had ravaged less directly – in Great Britain above all – the ruling class was tarred with failure: failure to prevent the war and failure to cope with the depression of the thirties.

Traditional rulers had moreover lost their monopoly of superior education. They were on the contrary suspected of being poorly versed in the crucial subjects of economics and modern physics. To put it bluntly, it was doubtful if they knew what they were talking about or if they were addressing themselves intelligently to what mattered most;* and disdain of this kind united the liberal professions with the young. It was accentuated by the decline of the American presidency into a chilling ineptitude and curdling vapidity which stripped it of the respect earned by Washington and Lincoln and many more. Ruling classes everywhere were portrayed – with the exaggerations but also the valid strokes of the caricature – as an elite with the wrong values and the

* Notably in economic matters where professional politicians who were also amateur economists caused unnecessary damage by being ignorant of the extent of their ignorance.

wrong priorities. Secretive and quite often corrupt, they emerged as a new version of Europe's *anciens régimes*.

Scientists – the priests and seers of the nuclear age – contributed to this critique, not least by being themselves divided. While some of the most eminent, such as Edward Teller, applauded every development of nuclear weaponry, others cast grave doubts not only on its propriety but also on the claims made for the working efficiency and accuracy of the new weapons. To the outsider and non-expert it seemed that the experts and those who swallowed their advice did not know as much as they claimed to know and did not know enough to make the use of their discoveries safe. Thus leading scientists as well as prominent statesmen were accused of rushing recklessly forward with their eyes half closed. Moreover modern science gave a new twist to a perennial target for radical indignation: capitalism. In his farewell speech on quitting the presidency in 1961 Eisenhower gave a warning against the 'unwarranted influence' of the alliance between capitalists and the military. In addition capitalists were attacked for recklessly polluting the environment, endangering human life and despoiling the natural world by the greed which led them to subordinate safeguards to profits. This anti-capitalist note with its obvious appeal to the marxist and non-marxist left and its linkage of the dangers of war with the dangers to life in peacetime substantially expanded the popular base of the protests of these decades.★

★ Capitalists had been a target for earlier generations of peace campaigners who reviled the captains of the arms industry as merchants of death. Theirs was a comparatively small section of capitalist industry but the ever increasing industrialisation of war gave birth to the 'military-industrial complex' not only geared to war production but also dominating the entire economy and so impinging unhealthily on government. The role of modern capitalism is complex. On the one hand it is a force for growth and for unification, if only because of its appetite for the fruits of size and monopoly. It also craves for order, but its order is the rule of power and not the rule of law. Law is frequently treated by capitalists as part of a hostile environment to be circumvented by hiring crafty lawyers, bankers and accountants. The order desired by modern capitalism is more akin to the autocratic side of the Roman empire than its jurisprudential: more order than law. While the Roman empire deserved its reputation for orderliness – far more so than the Roman republic in which the temple of Janus, the outward and visible sign of peace, was closed only twice

The temper of this period was greatly influenced by a coincidence: the Anglo-French attack on Egypt in collusion with Israel and the Soviet invasion of Hungary, both in 1956. These events outraged many people and the second played a considerable part in ensuring that the politics of protest would not be pro-Soviet. Hardly less formative was MacCarthyism in the United States which began – even before Vietnam – to transform the American image from liberal, pacific and anti-colonial to mindless, militant and offensive. These alignments, and the concurrent politicization of the rising generation, meshed with the nuclear revolution which was perceived as a transformation at least as profound as – and driven at much more headlong speed than – the combined industrial and democratic revolutions of the eighteenth and nineteenth centuries.

The promise of nuclear power was at first seen as both good and bad. Nuclear weapons were obviously abhorrent but 'atoms for peace' were on balance good. This sheer divide was, however, much modified as time went on and the generators of nuclear power for civil uses turned out to be as potentially lethal as bombs. Governments were suspected of being less than candid about what they knew or did not know about the safety of nuclear reactors, particularly after the enormous rises in the prices of imported oil during the seventies prompted them to accelerate the generation of nuclear power with, in the opinion of some scientists, incontinent speed and scant safeguards. Committees of the knowledgeable, the suspicious and the disgruntled mushroomed; signatures were collected in hundreds and thousands; in 1977 controversy over a nuclear plant at Malville in south-eastern France led to something like local battles; and in West Germany environmentalists, the Greens, concerned about toxic effluents – as well as acid rain, lead in petrol or simply the disfigurement of the countryside – won seats in the Bundestag and so pushed the politics of protest from the streets to the council chamber. This movement of alarm was dramatized and substantiated by the acci-

---

between the 7th century BC and the triumph of Augustus at Actium – the imperial order was not to everybody's liking or benefit. Modern capitalism likewise has contrived to be successful without becoming popular, a good thing for those in the right places.

dent in 1979 at the nuclear generator at Three Mile Island at Harrisburg, Pennsylvania, when claims and counter-claims about the extent of the threat under which the people of the area had been living could not conceal the fact that there was a threat of a peculiarly nasty kind. The alarm and distrust were magnified within a few years by the disaster at Chernobyl in 1986 which was not only appalling in itself but showed how carelessness or accident in one country might affect its neighbours. In western Europe Germans began to complain about Austrian and French threats to their safety, while in Britain controversy over Winscale (renamed Sellafield) went on and on and it took Chernobyl to persuade those in authority to promise candour in place of secrecy.

Yet nuclear weapons were a far greater source of disquiet than nuclear generators with the result that the core of popular protest was disarmament and specifically nuclear disarmament. Neither superpower used nuclear weapons but in Vietnam the United States used modern methods of mass destruction of comparable, if localized, horribleness. For some years therefore protest against the Vietnam war had a greater urgency, particularly within the United States, than campaigns against nuclear weapons. But the two protests – the one against a particular war and the other against a particular kind of war – engaged the same people, to the exclusion largely of protest against war as such.

III

The wartime A-bomb, which was developed in New Mexico and dropped on Japan, was followed in 1950 by the H-bomb. The Soviet Union was not far behind the United

States while in Great Britain the determination to become a third nuclear power, originally kept secret, was revealed in the mid-fifties and commended by the government as a way of maintaining Great Britain's eminence in the world and of getting a powerful armoury comparatively cheaply and without conscription. This policy was attacked as both fraudulent and vainglorious: fraudulent because nuclear weapons did not appear cheaper than non-nuclear, vainglorious because – despite Suez (which had few of the chauvinistic echoes of the Falklands war two decades later) – the British public was no longer keen for its government to run the world. The Labour Party, which had set the country on its postwar nuclear course, did not join in this attack which therefore developed outside parliament.

Two popular organisations were created in 1957. The first concentrated on stopping nuclear tests. It evolved from local groups in prosperous, middle-class areas of north west London and took the name of the National Council for the Abolition of Nuclear Weapons Tests (NCANWT). It was later merged in the Campaign for Nuclear Disarmament (CND), founded in 1958. The second organisation was the Direct Action Committee against Nuclear War (DAC). It too gave priority to stopping tests, financed an expedition to the Pacific to obstruct tests and organised the annual Easter protest marches to the Atomic Weapons Research Establishment at Aldermaston.

The aims of these organisations broadly converged but their methods were different. Both opposed nuclear testing and the presence of nuclear weapons, British or foreign, on British soil or in British territorial waters. Both were non-violent but CND was in addition opposed to illegality with the results that co-operation was edgy and CND itself spawned a more militant offshoot, the Committee of 100, which was closer to DAC than to its own parent. Differences over the propriety and effectiveness of mass civil disobedience, as practised by both DAC and the Committee of 100, were sharpened by personality clashes and to some extent by a generation gap. CND's leaders were middle-class, middle-aged (or elderly) socialists – J. B. Priestley, Bertrand Russell, Canon John Collins, Kingsley Martin, backed by an impressive array of well known writers, artists and thinkers and a larger host of unknown middle-class family folk who gave demonstration the air of a picnic. (Although intellectuals have been prominent in protest movements, most intellectuals join none.) A significant minority were Christians of various attachment but only half the Christians were pacifists. A minority within the peace movement was more politically engaged, more determined, more embittered. The minority accused the majority of being timorous and ineffective; the majority accused the minority of alienating more people than they persuaded.

CND came nearest to influencing events when the Labour Party's annual conference voted in 1960 in favour of abandoning British nuclear weapons and removing American ones. But the authority of a conference resolution over Labour MPs or a Labour government was unclear and contentious and by the time Labour returned to office in 1964 conference had reversed its anti-nuclear and unilateralist position. In these same years external events took the steam out of the peace movement. Whereas the Berlin crisis of 1961 exacerbated fears of war, the peaceful resolution of the Cuba crisis in 1962 together with the signing in 1963 of the Partial Test Ban Treaty reduced the temperature and stalled the disarmament movement. The authorities took energetic and even brutal action against demonstrators at the Holy Loch and other nuclear bases; hundreds were arrested and the Official Secrets Act was invoked in an attempt to give the movement a dangerous and subversive appearance. By the mid-sixties CND had faded away and the Committee of 100 dissolved itself in 1968. In so far as the public at large could be said to have passed judgement it had sensed that the unilateral renunciation of nuclear weapons was incompatible with membership of Nato and had opted in favour of the latter. Nato, an inescapably nuclear alliance, was at this date an irremovable piece of the political scene, because Europeans remained afraid of the Soviet Union.

The decline of CND in Great Britain coincided with the intensification of the war in Vietnam which became, outside the United States as well as within, the main focus for the peace movement. During the early sixties American attempts to play no more than a supporting role in the war manifestly failed. Military support was increased but the South Vietna-

mese were still the losing side. The Americans took control
and by 1968 had forces exceeding half a million in the
country, but still could not prevail. In the early seventies
ancillary operations against Laos and Cambodia added to the
death and destruction without bringing promise of victory.
By the time a cease-fire was signed at the beginning of 1973
the Americans had both suffered defeat and had been seen
to use the most sickening methods (including napalm and
the defoliating agent orange), contravening the laws of war
and the laxest dictates of humanity – methods which classical
Jus in Bello would have condemned as disproportionate.

The revulsion in the United States was moral and pointed.
It was moral inasmuch as it was directed against the way the
war was being fought and not against the failure to win it;
and it was pointed because the protesters were attacking their
own government over which, in a democratic society, they
claimed to have some control. Protest was strong among
middle-class, well educated young people who, like their
peers in western Europe, were already politically aroused by
other causes; and, like the British CND, it was anti-war
without being specifically pacifist. The pacifists among the
protesters found themselves engulfed in something larger
than themselves.

Their achievement was at best ragged. The war was
stopped but not primarily by organised protest. Pacifism has
been no stronger in the United States than in Europe. This
may surprise Americans who have been censorious of
Europe's divisive wars and predatory imperialism, and Europeans who think of the North American continent as an
area that has been spared war and its stirring emotions. But
immediately after Pearl Harbour in December 1941 Americans were almost unanimously in favour of war (96% – but
they had no choice); the pacifist churches did a somersault
and peace groups disintegrated. Four years later only 10%
disapproved of the atomization of Hiroshima and Nagasaki
but first reactions changed abruptly with the realisation of
what had been done and what it portended. Then the Cold
War and the Korean War effectively mothballed the peace
movement in spite of the emergence of a New Left which criticised Truman for mishandling relations with the Soviet
Union and 'starting' the Cold War. The New Left was even

more censorious of the Truman administration on the domestic front where it was accused of betraying Roosevelt's New Deal and paying scant attention to civil rights, the Deep South and urban ghettos. The New Left was itself always more an intellectual enclave than a popular movement; it sounded too socialist and rasping and eventually succumbed to the splintering malady of the Left everywhere.*

Popular concern about radioactivity and nuclear testing was stirred when tests in the Pacific in 1954 killed some Japanese fishermen as well as poisoning vast numbers of fish and infecting an area of 7,000 square miles. In 1958 the *Golden Rule* sailed into the danger zone round Eniwetok atoll in order to stop or at least publicise further tests; the captain and his crew were arrested and imprisoned. A second vessel containing a non-political anthropologist and his family also sailed by coincidence into the forbidden area. The campaign to stop tests, which had the support of Adlai Stevenson in the presidential election of 1952, was both a protest against nuclear weapons as such and a protest against tests conducted with inadequate safeguards or knowledge.

The next decade – the sixties – saw the beginnings of a student protest which swelled to the proportions of massive student revolt. In 1968 parts of the University of Columbia were both closed by the authorities and occupied by students; 628 students were arrested, some of them radical members of the SDS (Student for a Democratic Society, founded in 1962) but others were of a more middling persuasion who were increasingly making common cause with the radicals notwithstanding the outrage caused to many by violent SDS tactics. At Berkeley in California there were battles and hundreds of other campuses followed suit more or less obstreporously. Their catalogue of grievances covered university curricula, teacher selection and competence, university administration and rules of behaviour (particularly sexual). In 1969 the National Guard entered the University of Wisconsin with fixed bayonets and arrested a number of

---

* It was to some extent rescued by hysteria on the Right – for example, the John Birch Society, founded in 1958 after a two-day speech to an audience of eleven (the society called Eisenhower a communist), or the creation in 1959 of the Minutemen pledged to take arms at a minute's notice to thwart a communist take-over of the state.

students as helicopters patrolled overhead. The SDS and its more extreme offshoot, the Weathermen, had succeeded in one thing: creating alarm. The FBI and CIA, each pretty much a law unto itself (and therefore in student eyes exempted from law), set spies in what they regarded as a nation-wide revolutionary force and the army used agents, wiretaps and various illicit provocations against civilians and churches as well as within its own ranks. (These activities were later investigated by a Senate sub-committee under Senator Sam T. Ervin which failed to get all relevant information but revealed a disturbing disregard for the law on the part of the authorities responsible for law-keeping.)

The disorders across the country – a fusion of grievances about education, more general attacks on the government's social policies or lack of them, and hostility to the war in Vietnam – were exacerbated by President Nixon's choleric response. In 1968 Nixon's one virtue was that he might, if elected, stop the war. But he did not and his promise to withdraw forces from Vietnam turned into an invasion of Cambodia. He described students indiscriminately as 'bums', his vice president Spiro Agnew made a series of equally outrageous remarks, and his Attorney-General referred to university administrators as 'stupid bastards'. Leadership of this quality touched its chilling nadir when Nixon stigmatised as 'incipient revolution' demonstrations against the bombing of Cambodia in which, in May 1970, six students at Kent State and Jackson State Universities were killed by the National Guard.* While the Left tried to represent the university authorities as part of a right-wing conspiracy, Nixon, Agnew and their like claimed the support of the so-called silent majority which occupied the middle ground but a special commission appointed by Nixon to investigate campus unrest (the Scranton Commission) reported that there would be no peace on the campuses until there was

* These deaths were later described as unjustified and unreasonable over-reaction. The issue was reopened in 1973. An Ohio State grand jury refused to indict members of the Ohio National Guard but a Federal grand jury did so. The judge ruled that there was no evidence of a conspiracy to deprive the victims of their constitutional rights and the accused were discharged. Civil suits were unsuccessful. The Governor of Ohio and the Federal Attorney-General were suspected of a concerted cover-up.

peace in Vietnam. The Commission managed to blame just about everybody but pinpointed the President's fault in dividing instead of uniting the nation. Nixon, however, remained confident that he was setting a moral tone against 'cancerous' elements in American society and confident too that there were votes in being offensive to students. When Chancellor Alexander Heard of Vanderbilt University, Nixon's special presidential adviser on student affairs, told the President that he – Nixon – understood neither the nature nor the gravity of the student – and teacher – revolt, Nixon publicly rejected his analysis, made a series of speeches blaming university authorities and a minority of so-called terrorists, told the universities to put their houses in order and asked Congress for funds to recruit a thousand extra FBI agents to combat violence and arson.

The temper of these years was violent, in deed as well as word. One of the most immediate issues for many of the young was obedience to the law. Conscription had been continuous from 1940 except for 13 months in 1947–48 when it was discontinued in the false belief that volunteers would be numerous enough: the largest annual call-up was 380,000 in 1966. During the Vietnam war 75,000 deserted or dodged the draft and thousands were dishonourably discharged. The motives of the recalcitrants are impossible to disentangle. Cowardice must have played some part, even though that may be a harsh term for the refusal to face death in a remote and squalidly fought war. Genuine pacifism was also a motive but probably the strongest element in the refusal to serve was indignation against the kind of war that developed, the deceptions practised on the public by politicians and generals, and the recourse to 'dirty tricks' by a profession in which young people had enlisted in the expectation of an honourable career.

The war made a contribution to American law on the right of conscientious objection. In 1970 a court ruled that religious belief was not an essential pre-requisite (*US vs. Walsh*) but in the next year the Supreme Court affirmed by eight to one that exemption was available only to those who objected to all war and not to those opposed to a particular war. Two of the defendants before the Court argued that the Vietnam war was an unjust war but the Court upheld

the army's refusal to release them. One of them, a Roman
Catholic, testified that he would be willing to fight in a war
of national self-defence or to serve in a UN peace force. He
was not exempted. Nixon, who had promised in his election
campaign to be 'very liberal', refused to amnesty deserters
and dodgers. To many Americans they were simply traitors.
President Ford, having given Nixon a pardon for his hardly
less heinous crimes against his presidential oath, introduced
a complicated review scheme under which deserters might
be pardoned in return for alternative service for two years or
less and reaffirmation of their allegiance. No comprehensive
pardon was issued and although opposed from various angles
Ford's scheme was marginally approved by public opinion
as a way of burying an embarrassing problem.

The end of the war, coupled with the Watergate scandals
and Nixon's dishonourable discharge from the presidency,
shifted the limelight but the war left a permanent mark on
European attitudes to the United States and therefore to
Nato and its nuclear strategies. Europe's latent anti-Americanism, a mixture of jealousy and intellectual snobbery
nourished by the crasser aspects of American materialism
and economic dominion, was sharpened by the conduct of
a war which was the biggest offence against peace since the
Second World War. A war between the Superpowers would
have been a greater catastrophe but it did not happen. There
were plenty of other wars, notably in the Middle East, as
well as brutal acts of aggression involving, notably in Afghanistan, fearful misery and slaughter, but the war in Vietnam
with its adjuncts in Laos and Cambodia dominated the
imagination. It fuelled opposition to the American military
presence which had once been a welcome protection against
a Soviet menace, undermined the American title to military
and moral leadership of the western alliance and turned
American weapons in Europe into symbols of suspect militancy and political unpredictability. It sanctified protest –
against American leaders, against modern war.

IV

In the seventies the Nato alliance was becoming an irritant in western European politics. It was, however, held together by Soviet beastliness. The glimmer of something less awful than Stalinism (which was a feature of Khrushchev's wayward rule) had been extinguished under Brczhnev and although Soviet external aggression inspired decreasing fear in western Europe, it was easy for anti-Soviet propogandists to maintain Europe's traditional distaste for the barbarous state on its eastern flank. At the end of the decade the Soviet invasion of Afghanistan and – more pertinently – Moscow's modernisation of its theatre of nuclear weaponry in Europe confirmed Europe's anti-Soviet sentiments, but almost simultaneously the western response in weaponry revived the anti-nuclear campaign and anti-Americanism.

The key point, although not the first point, in this revival was the election of Ronald Reagan as President of the United States. In external affairs Reagan stood, with minor inconsistencies, for peace by domination. The forces to be dominated were the Soviet Union and anything else that the rampant right might choose to label communist or 'marxist'. This Manichaean and simplistic *Weltanschauung* made the Reagan administration soft on tyrannies provided they were anti-communist (South Africa, President Ferdinand Marcos, Latin American strong men) and it proclaimed a casuistical distinction between totalitarian regimes which were bad – and on the left – and authoritarian regimes which were acceptable allies – and on the right. This moral juggling was coupled with a tough stance on Superpower arms negotiations and with arms programmes designed to put the United States in a different category from the Soviet Union: a policy for victory, not accommodation. These attitudes were anathema to the left and also profoundly disturbing to middling and even right-wing opinion in Europe which regarded the President's pronouncements as silly and his policies as dangerous. There appeared once more a basis for a broad coalition of protest. CND came back to life.

Paradoxically the central issue which prompted its resurgence had initially nothing to do with Reagan although Reagan's sayings and doings gave it extra stuffing. This issue was the deployment in Europe by Nato of new weapons, Cruise and Pershing II.

These weapons were a response to the appearance on the Soviet side of the SS20 which, from 1977 onwards, replaced the SS4s and 5s first deployed in 1960. The SS20 had a far more formidable range and throw-power but its true strategic significance was minimal since it left intact the American long range deterrent which, together with its Soviet opposite, maintained the peace by mutual deterrence. The deployment of the SS20 was therefore a blunder, which was compounded when the western allies, looking down the barrels of the SS20, cast around for a counter-move. President Carter sensibly proposed a further reinforcement of the submarine element in the long range deterrent, but from the European point of view these weapons had the disadvantage of being invisible and so European leaders pressed the Americans to station in their countries an evident riposte to the SS20. The Cruise/Pershing programme, as militarily irrelevant as the SS20, was thus adopted by Nato before Reagan's election.

This programme was, however, more than irrelevant. It was also unpopular and the European leaders who promoted it found themselves in trouble with sections of their own electorates – the more so when endemic anti-Americanism was fuelled by anti-Reaganism and the campaign against Cruise and Pershing was turned into a fresh vote of no confidence in the United States. In Great Britain the arguments of the 1960s for unilateral action on nuclear weapons were resuscitated, with the same force – and the same flaws.

Unilateralism did not mean a dismantling of the American long range deterrent without compensation on the Soviet side. It comprised two layers: first, a disbelief in the genuineness of American intentions to negotiate mutual disarmament with the Soviet Union; secondly, and consequently, a refusal by a particular partner in the alliance to have nuclear weapons on its soil or in its waters. The disbelief was widespread but the refusal – the active nub of protest – was much less widely endorsed because it entailed a breach of the conditions of any partnership, an assertion of one partner's right to ignore his partners' wishes, and so ultimately a readiness to quit the partnership. The readiness was not there. Unpopular the Americans might be, but not as unpopular as that because they were still an irreplaceable part of the anti-Soviet stance and – equally important although far less often formulated – because the United States was incontrovertibly a democracy where the people could change the policies. This therefore was a tacit acknowledgement that a popular protest movement must in the end rely on the strength of protest within the ambit of the government whose doings evoked that protest. American protest might influence the course of the Vietnam war or of arms talks between the Superpowers; foreign protesters, however, were in such issues all but ineffective.

A direct consequence was division in the protesters' ranks. In Great Britain the Anti-Nuclear Campaign (ANC) was prepared to envisage secession from Nato and may even have wanted it on mixed emotional and rational grounds: emotional anti-Reaganism and the reasoned (although feeble) argument that Great Britain non-allied would escape from the Soviet nuclear threat. Other groups were repelled by the ANC's political bias and weak reasoning. So two main streams took shape. The one embraced the old but minor communist Left, the New Left (a potpourri of groups inside and outside the Labour party but generally on or to the left of it) and the proponents of general disarmament; the other consisted of CND veterans together with the ecologist lobby. The correspondence columns of *The Times* and the formation of local groups all over the country testified to the reinvigoration of debate with unilateralism at its centre. Distrust of government policies and, an insistent note, government candour was manifest. In September 1980 a poll showed that nearly half the population (48%) expected nuclear war in their lifetime, nearly three-quarters (70%) considered that the threat had grown, but fewer than a third (30%) wanted unilaterally to down British nuclear arms. A protest march in London in October assembled some 50,000 demonstrators. Although pressures were building up again in Great Britain before Reagan succeeded Carter in the White

House, in the year after that event CND more than doubled
its membership and a demonstration in London in October
1981 was three times the size of the previous year's. Some
local government authorities demonstrated their support for
the anti-nuclear movement by declaring their bailiwicks to
be nuclear-free zones or by refusing to spend money for civil
defence against nuclear attack (thus contravening a central
government pamphlet *Protect and Survive* which was not only
out of date technically but also as ludicrous in its own way
as the concept of a nuclear-free borough council). Central
government retaliated by alleging that CND was massively
infiltrated by communists and other politically motivated
and subversive tools of Moscow. CND was periodically
worried about communist enthusiasts who tried (unsuccessfully) to take over local branches and the organisation, while
overtly anti-American, remained persistently anti-Soviet.

The logical consequence of anti-nuclear protest was the
demand for the abolition of nuclear weapons. But abolition-
ists were confronted by a tough obstacle in the blind march
of invention. Nuclear weapons could not be disinvented and
although it is not utterly impossible to abolish something
that exists it is exceedingly painful to do so when somebody
else possesses it, most risky in the case of arms. In the last
quarter of the century peace movements had narrowed their
programmes to disarmament, more particularly, nuclear
disarmament, and in doing so set themselves a formidable
task. Although their numbers gave them, in democratic
countries, more political consequence than the solitary
pacifist, their contribution to peace was not demonstrably
greater. They had a marginal impact in marginal seats when
elections came round, but since no major party was pacifist
or had so far even offered in office any markedly different
defence policy, this parliamentary impact was slight. Their
extra-parliamentary activities, however healthy in democratic terms, were no more immediately effective and raised
furthermore large questions about the propriety of some of
their methods as well as the desirability of their aims – to
which questions we shall revert in a later chapter. Protesters
were once more caught in a trap, faced with the choice
between two kinds of action: the unproductive and the coun-
ter-productive.

PART II

TODAY

8

Attitudes

It is broadly plausible to judge that civilised society, sporadically but increasingly, has come to denounce war and even to equate the civilised condition with the repudiation of war: the *condition humaine* becomes civilised as it purges itself of violence. But this view is neither self-evident nor universal. When Thomas Hobbes wrote (Leviathan, i, 4) that 'the condition of war . . . is a condition of war of everyone against everyone' he was making what he believed to be a factual assertion and implied that the denunciation of war is a waste of breath. Others have proclaimed the positive glories of war, Othello for example: 'The quality, Pride, pomp and circumstance of glorious war' (Othello, III, 3). Yet others have been simply resigned to its occurrence in the hope that perhaps in some mysterious way war brings benefit as well as pain:

> "But what good came of it at last?"
> Quoth little Peterkin.
> "Why, that I cannot tell" said he,
> "But 'twas a famous victory."
> (Robert Southey, *The Battle of Blenheim*)

These views can be multiplied many times over in every age. They are part of what pacifists have to contend with: hostility, indifference, the feeling of helplessness. It is evident that not everybody hates war or thinks it worthwhile to join the effort to prevent it.

'Stopping war,' wrote Thomas Merton, the American Trappist and poet (1915–69), 'requires enormous effort of will and thought.' But who can make this effort with any prospect of success? And what is it that has to be done?

The pacifist cannot do anything. His role is not to do but to be. But it is immensely important that he continue to be. He sees to it that we preserve the ideal of peace. He stands on the line between civilisation and barbarism. Without him society crosses that line. His kind are the quintessential martyrs, often derided and disregarded but never entirely snuffed out. He proclaims the supreme value of peace even though he cannot ensure it. For this ineffectiveness he is not to be belittled because without him the impulse to keep the peace could be lost. But pacifism seeks to change human nature and that cannot be done within a political timescale. Human nature is constantly changing with genetic mutations and environmental pressures but these are fearfully slow. In the foreseeable future human nature has to be taken as virtually static so that the political problem consists, not in changing it as the pacifist would do, but in accepting and trying to constrain it.

I do not believe that in this context there is anything else to be said about that honourable and admirable figure, the pacifist.

Peace groups or movements are another matter. They have a role, active and political, which is entirely different from holding the mirror of virtue before the face of the beast; and they have this role by virtue of their symbiotic relationship with governments. Keeping the peace has two main ingredients: the skills of statesmen (by which complimentary term I mean those who constitute the governments of states) and the pressures upon them.

So long as wars are waged by states, statesmen are the protagonists of peace. But statesmen are also the embodiment of the state's interests and of its propensity to go to any lengths, including war, to advance and defend those interests. Consequently statesmen, whose business it is to juggle with ends and means, need to be strengthened or restrained, advised or threatened, by voices from outside their small circles.

These voices are not welcome and may be easily suppressed; one of the main functions and benefits of democracy is to allow them to be heard and weighed. They are diverse. On the one hand are the relatively small, closely knit, bodies of special pleaders who are not essentially hostile to governments but are primarily guided by the peculiar values which they have inherited and cherish: churchmen and lawyers, for example. On the other hand there is the more distrustful, more impolite or raucous, more numerous but also more amorphous throng who, in the particular circumstances of a particular state, may be able to affect the thinking and actions of statesmen or even (in democracies) throw them out: electorates, pressure groups, broad protest movements. Their function is to constrain or propel.

All these forces inside or close to or beyond the inner circle of government operate within the special fears and circumstances of their time. In the second half of the twentieth century two new factors predominate: the advent of nuclear weapons which has aggravated the horrors of war, and the proliferation of the sovereign state which has multiplied the occasions for it. The one has sharpened ethical and legal questions about the rightfulness of war and the use of certain weapons; the other has complicated practical questions about how to settle international disputes without war.

These are the traditional concerns of churches and lawyers. In addition the two factors together – but particularly the first – alarm people at large and incite them to express their alarm, to criticise their governments and to propound their favoured remedies by speech or writing or action, any of which may break the law.

Nuclear weapons dominate the scene owing to their unprecedented lethal capacity and psychological impact. But they have been, and still are, in the possession of very few states, and even though the few are becoming more they remain a small minority of the totality (161) of states in existence today. Nuclear weapons operate as a deterrent to wars of unprecedented force but they are irrelevant in most warlike situations. They have opened a gap between one kind of war and another. Where there used to be a continuous spectrum from great wars to trivial ones, all of them waged with similar weapons, there is now a distinction in kind between nuclear and non-nuclear wars and a corresponding discrepancy in preventive measures and in attitudes to war. Wars within the nuclear circle are mightily deterred but other wars are no more, and no differently, deterred than they used to be.

The occasions for non-nuclear wars have been suddenly multiplied by the dissolution of the European world empires within the span of a single generation. If, as is undoubtedly the case, the principal agents of war are sovereign states, then the increase in the number of these warmakers makes war more likely. The number of quarrels which now rank as international disputes has been magnified. Furthermore, the machinery for resolving such disputes without war has been complicated qualitatively as well as quantitatively. This machinery, now embodied mainly in the United Nations, has been developed upon the assumption that the states which are members of the international organisation have enough in common – in their past and in their aims – to constitute a community in which they will for most of the time submit to rules of conduct formulated by them and enacted in binding contractual form. But the existence of such a community is for the time being questionable because the number and variety of the members of the UN has seriously diminished their community; in which case the state, whether a new state or an old one, is less restrained than it was a hundred years ago before the construction of the United Nations. One of the important underlying conundrums of today is whether this attenuation of the community of states is a passing phenomenon or not.

There is, finally, a third feature of our time which, although not new, has an importance similar to the two novelties just mentioned. This is the warmaking determination and warmaking capacity of substantial organised groups which are not states but which war on states. Unlike criminal organisations such as drug traffickers or city fraudsters, they aim not to circumvent the laws of a state but to harm the state itself or even (in the extreme case of the PLO) to destroy it. By arrogating to themselves the right to make war in defiance of the state's cherished right to a monopoly of legitimate belligerence, these groups cut across the neat and tidy demarcation between states and non-states. States and statesmen riposte by describing them as terrorists and so seek, by mere words, to reduce them to the category of common criminals or outlaws. But this is no more than a

semantic response which confuses the issue by lumping together serious and substantial organisations such as the PLO
or ANC with incoherent or transient gangs with no claim
to recognition as anything else. The former have added to
the repertory of war and it is no good pretending that what
they do is not war. They raise therefore the question whether
their actions should be brought within the international laws
relating to armed conflict.

So we have a panorama of war. There is, first, war
between Superpowers which, however it may begin, is most
likely to become nuclear sooner rather than later. There is
war between Superpowers fought by proxy, in intention at
least non-nuclear. There is war by a nuclear state against a
non-nuclear. There is war – the commonest variety – in
which neither protagonist possesses nuclear weapons and
neither has a nuclear backer prepared to alter the terms of
the struggle by supplying nuclear weapons. There is, finally,
war by or against a non-state. But within this panorama two
broad categories are again distinguishable: the nuclear and
the non-nuclear. The imagination, if nothing else, makes
them so. The law of *Jus in Bello* distinguishes too between
wars waged in one way or another but the peculiar impact
of nuclear war is upon the imagination rather than codes;
and while the lawyer's main preoccupation remains war as
such, the churchman and moralist are easily seduced by the
horrors of nuclear war into turning a technical category into
a moral one.

II

Whenever war becomes especially shocking the ethical
response to it becomes sharper. This process may be dated

from the first *levées en masse*, or the revealed horrors of the
Crimean and Franco-Prussian wars (depicted in *The Times*
and Emile Zola's *La Débacle*), or the squalid slaughter of the
First World War, or the mass destructiveness of the Second.
The starting point is immaterial; it could be set much earlier
since the main agent of both destructiveness and revulsion
is each generation's newly invented killing machine.

With the advent of nuclear weapons, the acme so far of
the application of scientific and industrial skills to warfare,
a new theological note has been added to the growing moral
disquiet. This is the argument that there is something peculiarly sinful about man's capacity to destroy God's entire
creation – an odd argument, it may be thought, since it
appears to overlook God's power to re-create what He
created in the first place and, in addition, His possible
grounds for willing a purge of the earth even more complete
than that which He effected in Noah's time.

Theological argument apart, churches, when roused, are
natural leaders of moral debate. Although well established
churches have a tendency to torpor, they are from time to
time retrieved from it when, like Milton's fallen angel, they
witness 'huge affliction and dismay'. Mass slaughter – or
extremes of cruelty or poverty – prod them to righteous
indignation (which, according to another poet, Blake, is the
voice of God) and expostulation. Even before the nuclear
bombing of Japanese cities the raids on, for example,
Hamburg and Dresden – more horrible than earlier German
attacks on British cities because, coming later in the war,
they employed bigger aircraft and bigger bombs and, at
Dresden, were unopposed – demonstrated how far medieval
notions of proportionality, economy of force and immunity
of civilians have been left behind. In the aftermath of Hiroshima and Nagasaki the churches have been forced to address
themselves once more to traditional questions in nuclear
dress: whether the Christian commitment to peace and non-
violence overrides the state's determination to defend itself
with nuclear weapons; whether the use of these weapons can
in any circumstances be justified; whether mere possession
of them, and consequently a policy of nuclear deterrence,
are compatible with Christian teaching (whether, that is, a
moral purpose – peace or self-defence – may legitimately be

pursued by inherently immoral means); and whether a nuclear power ought to divest itself of nuclear weapons unilaterally or only by agreement with its adversaries.

Pope Pius XII declared all nuclear weapons to be immoral if the consequences of their use were so extreme as to pass beyond human control – a pronouncement which, albeit hypothetical and to that extent ambiguous, laid stress on human responsiblity. Even the fight against injustice and the legitimate defence of possessions had to be renounced if it ran the risk of causing total annihilation in a given area. Pope John XXII's encyclical *Pacem in Terra* appears to condemn all war waged to redress wrongs but not wars of self-defence: it makes, he says, 'no sense to maintain that war is a fit instrument to repair violation of justice'. The second Vatican Council urged the creation of a system to avoid wars (an attempt therefore to limit its sources) and condemned unequivocally the destruction of entire cities and large populated areas as a crime against God and man. In the United States, where Cardinal Griffin opined as early as 1955 that the use of the H-bomb conflicted with Christian principles, the Roman Catholic and other churches have shown uneasiness about getting left out of a debate with evident ethical and theological connotations. (Nor may they prudently leave protest marches, which often have the air of pilgrimages, to Baptists and atheists.) More recently the Roman Catholic bishops in the United States, displaying more spiritual perturbation than logical rigour, have argued for a no-first-use declaration (which removes most of the deterrence from the deterrent) and have opposed any targeting which would intentionally kill civilians (which nuclear warheads make inevitable).

Protestants have been similarly cautious and puzzled. Karl Barth stigmatised war as fundamentally anti-Christian but could conceive of a war commanded or sanctioned by God; although vigorously opposed to war, he could envisage a war as permissibly ruthless and even total. Reinhold Niebuhr, in the pessimistic-realistic tradition, regarded war as ineradicable and was scornful of a liberal protestantism tinged with visions of the perfectability of man. As his book *Moral Man and Immoral Society* showed, he regarded societies as inherently immoral (but individuals as capable of improvement), so that force is rational and necessary and non-violence is applicable only in special circumstances (such as those which Gandhi confronted in British India). Violence might be positively laudable against some evils, although the definition of these evils changes: nazism and communism take the place of the barbarism against which St Augustine blessed the arms of the Roman state. What may be done depends upon whom it is done to and how: war may still be just provided the cause is good and the force limited. This is sound – but anachronistic – medieval theology, firmly grounded in the antithesis between right and wrong, virtue and sin – and in man's ability to distinguish the one from the other.

Different problems arise when the elements in the balance are social and well as ethical. In Great Britain, not a strikingly religious country but one with as strong a social conscience as may be found, basic moral worries have been accentuated by social concern as the economic stringencies of the 1970s and 1980s have raised awkward questions about cutting social services in order to meet swelling military budgets. On the one hand a bishop of London has said that the use even of nuclear weapons might be justified, while other clerics have maintained that the nuclear age has made all wars unjustifiable. Unqualified opponents of nuclear weaponry denounce their mere possession but are unable to agree on how to get rid of them. A Church of England working party recommended in 1982 that Great Britain should cancel its decision to buy Trident (whose soaring costs were being fudged by the government), cancel the Chevaline programme for extending the life of Polaris missiles, phase out Polaris but not leave Nato. But these recommendations sidestep the crucial problem of what to do if a majority of the partners in Nato reject them.

The Christian opposition to war elevates one part of Christian teaching. When the churches go beyond assertion to inhibition – when, that is to say, they not only insist on the supreme value of peace and non-violence but also seek to stop the state from using or having certain weapons – they provoke the resentment of politicians and risk divisions in their own ranks. The failure, for example, of the Church of England to give full-throated applause to the outcome of the

Falklands war, its refusal to put the boasts of victory before the lament for the dead, evoked anger and surprise among political leaders who could not see that modern war has loosened the alliance between church and state. A supranational church escapes the immediate political difficulties: the church of Rome no longer has a Roman or any other empire to support. But an established church such as the Church of England, or nationally organised congregations such as most of the American churches, have to face embarrassing conflicts of loyalty and charges of unbecoming conduct. They recognise that the state has claims upon them ('Render unto Caesar . . .') but the extent of those claims is no longer so liberally interpreted. Christians try to strike a balance between support for the state and support for anti-war and anti-nuclear movements, but in doing so their voices are divided and their impact thereby lessened. Governments do not like opposition from churches – even Stalin was at pains in 1941 to get the Russian Orthodox Church on his side against the Germans – but so long as churches are ambivalent governments are able to discount clerical rebuke and portray churchmen as naively careless of the overriding claims of national security.

This critical ambiguity reflects more than divided counsels among the critics. It corresponds also to the strangely ambiguous nature of what is being criticised. Fear and condemnation of nuclear weaponry is focussed on the conflict between the Superpowers but the core of this conflict is peculiarly difficult to define. It does not fit into the familiar pattern of Great Power conflicts. It is morally monstrous not merely because of its nuclear threat but also because it seems unprecedentedly pointless: pointless slaughter is even more repellent than slaughter with an intelligible purpose.

Conflicts between states have habitually expressed themselves territorially. Initially the American-Soviet conflict adopted this pattern: it was a conflict over Germany which ended, or faded away, when neither side won a commanding position in central Europe and Germany itself was partitioned. Since that time the Superpower conflict has turned into a worldwide confrontation backed by nuclear weapons but increasingly expressed in ideological rather than territorial terms and so more propagandist than purposeful.

In so far as this conflict is not ideological – capitalist imperialism vs. communist imperialism – it is about the weapons themselves, thus converting the stockpile of instruments of war into the primary stuff of international competition. Counting warheads has become more significant than annexing territory. Yet war is not a way to add to the stockpile – on the contrary. So the question arises whether, behind the rhetorical allegations of rival imperialisms, there is something else or nothing at all. Is the Superpower conflict just a shouting match?

III

On the Soviet side the overriding aims of policy since the defeat of Germany in 1945 have been the security of the Soviet Union's European frontiers and getting equal and then keeping equal with the United States. The first of these aims was to have been achieved by dominating eastern and central Europe and by dominating or debilitating Germany. Eastern Europe, overrun during 1944 and 1945, was placed under the control of obedient communist henchmen but nationalism has proved stronger than communist elites and the one thing which might conceivably have reconciled these countries to Soviet domination – economic progress – failed them. The Soviet Union's management of its own economy has been inept (even allowing for the dreadful problems set by war), its interference in its neighbours' economies depredatory and obstructive. Moscow and its satraps alienated potential friends as well as ancient enemies, including in particular that most obdurate of oppositions, the peasantry. Even lackeys have begun to hedge their bets.

The Stalinist empire has moreover a peculiar weakness. Unlike western European empires Soviet imperialism is exercised in Europe over peoples who regard their masters as cultural inferiors whom they despise and have no wish to emulate. There exists nothing like the love-hate relationship between British and Indians or the reverence felt by many Asians and Africans for French civilisation. In spite of its scientific and technological achievements which command admiration the Soviet Union remains culturally as well as geographically on the European fringe, more isolated than any of the continent's earlier dominant powers.

The flaws in the Stalinist system have been made manifest by revolts at various points beginning in the year of Stalin's death (1953) until, in the 1980s, Moscow dared not intervene directly to prevent the overthrow of communist party rule in Poland. The political configuration of the area has been rendered uncertain with the military as the most likely heirs to discredited communist parties.

Stalin failed to extend Soviet rule to Germany and had to settle for a minor part of it. The larger part, moreover, staged a spectacular economic recovery, became the military nub of an anti-Soviet alliance and politically an ally of the United States more crucial for the Superpower confrontation than any other. Here too Stalin's long term plan did not work: Germany was not dominated and western Germany was not kept weak. And some time in this century or the next the question of the unification of Germany will again arise.

The second overriding aim of Soviet foreign policy since the Second World War has been military equivalence with the Americans. Although sometimes expressed as economic and material equivalence, this really means military equivalence. It has led to desperate measures such as the subordination of the domestic economy to the requirements of military science and stockpiles, to Khrushchev's insane attempt to plant Soviet missiles in the American hemisphere (for which he paid with his dismissal), and to self-defeating attempts to disrupt the American-European alliance by piling up theatre weapons aimed at European targets. The latter aspects of this policy have been fruitless but the Soviet Union has succeeded in making itself, if not the military equal of the United States, at least a power in the same class, possessing similar weapons in adequate quantities and extending its military reach from Europe to most of the world. Its military expenditure, although subject to some economic restraint, is unencumbered by popular protest and it has done well in the arms race, if in little else. It can deter the United States but its European security problem is back to where it was in 1945. Almost uniquely in the history of major powers it has not a friend in the world, thanks mainly to the ferocity of its domestic system and the consequent persistence of the idea that Russia is the uncivilised member of the European family. Finally, the nightmare of a Sino-American alliance has created for Moscow a security problem which is potentially although not yet actually as alarming as the American-European alliance.

Given these developments since the end of the Second World War, there appear to be two things that a Soviet government cannot tolerate: a reunification of Germany accompanied by the maintenance of the German-American alliance, and American action to accentuate the disintegration of Soviet control over eastern Europe or obstruct Soviet attempts to find a new security system to take the place of Stalin's. Either of these threats would be met by desperate measures, even perhaps to the point of dicing with the risk of nuclear war.

On the American side the principal aims of policy have been neither clear nor consistent. This is a consequence of being top dog, a position which leads to little beyond a determination to stay top dog and a preoccupation with the question whether one still is. The enormous economic preponderance of the United States, consolidated during the Second World War and maintained for a generation thereafter, coupled with geographical invulnerability to anything except suicidal Soviet attack, has robbed the United States of the normal incentives to ponder and formulate foreign political objectives. As a result American policies have been less concrete than sentimental and visionary. The outstanding example of this sentimentality is the virtually unconditional American support for Israel. This has been uncritically ascribed to the strength of the Jewish lobby in the United States but, without denying the effectiveness of this lobby, it may be doubted whether the Jewish community, concentrated in a relatively small number of areas, has the political power to hitch the United States to Israel's larger ambitions and more ruthless practices. There has been a second factor: a guilty American conscience about the way the American government refused, in spite of the evidence, to believe in or try to do anything about the mass murder of Europe's Jews during the war years. Americans were not alone in this wilful myopia but they have been alone in translating it into an enduring political obligation and the adoption of double standards in relation to Israel. American support for Israel is, revealingly, an attitude based on emotion rather than a policy based on rational calculation.

No less sentimental, and much more pertinent to the Superpower conflict, has been the American notion, mooted in the fifties and resurrected in the eighties, that the United States should rescue the peoples of eastern Europe from Soviet subjugation. This pious, vain hope, normally expressed in military terms, owes much to myth and guilt. At Yalta in February 1945, it has been argued by a number of historians (and non-historians), that Roosevelt failed to use American power to force Stalin to allow these peoples their freedom. Since by this date Stalin's armies were already in control (and had been so in some areas for a year or more) there was nothing Roosevelt could do beyond getting ambiguous promises from Stalin – and nothing Roosevelt's successors could do when the promises were broken except threaten the Soviet Union with war, a threat which was never realistic or seriously contemplated even before that country became a nuclear power. Nevertheless the American conscience has remained uneasy, and the existence in the United States of sizeable communities of Poles and other eastern Europeans, albeit far less influential than the Jewish lobby, keeps that conscience tender.

This conscience is not allied with any concrete political aim, for the United States has no thought of substituting an American for a Soviet imperium in eastern Europe. It is, however, allied with a powerful emotion: hatred of communism. Anti-communism is the nearest thing to a guiding theme in American postwar external policies, and for most of the time communism has meant Soviet communism:

Yugoslav and Chinese communists, once they turned against the Soviet Union, are transferred to a different category, while most other communists are classified as tools of Moscow. Hatred of the Soviet regime and of communist doctrines are easily understandable emotions, the one obnoxious to liberal America and the other to American capitalism and property-owners; but like conscience, they foster visionary longings, not policies. Americans would clearly love to see the destruction of the Soviet Union and the total eradication of communism throughout the world. But this apocalypse is not something that American policies can bring about.

Lacking concrete sources of conflict and material bones of contention both Superpowers concentrate necessarily on the modalities, not the stuff, of their antagonism. These modalities take the form of ideological rhetoric and the arms' race. There has been some manoeuvring for position in secondary zones but the effects have been negligible: the American war in Vietnam (a venture more anti-Chinese than anti-Soviet) has not altered the American-Soviet equation; nor has the replacement of American by Soviet influence in Ethiopia, or the reverse in Egypt, or the Soviet attempt to impose military instead of remote control over Afghanistan. What American and Soviet statesmen talk about, and what others see and condemn and fear, are above all their – nuclear – armaments.

The fears, arguably, are exaggerated. Nuclear war is an appalling prospect. The nuclear arms race is a fearfully expensive and idiotic way of conducting international relations. But a nuclear war is a much less likely event than non-nuclear wars (a number of which are usually going on at any time). Neither nuclear Superpower has any intention of going to war with the other, and the notion that wars happen by mistake has scant historical basis. The nuclear deterrent deters; it rules out war as a rational instrument of policy and is to that extent a stabilising element.*

The nuclear deterrent is unlike all pre-nuclear deterrents. The latter were one factor in calculating the pros and cons

* It does not rule out another Masada, whether by Israel or any other state. Samson can still pull the house down about his own and his enemies' ears.

of starting a war but they did not – other things being
sufficiently unequal – ultimately and on their own deter. The
nuclear deterrent does so deter by making all such calcu-
lations senseless. Furthermore, nobody knows enough about
the weapons to risk using them. What is known is that they
will kill millions and wreak unimaginable destruction; what
else they may do is more confidently asserted than known,
since rarely in the history of war have weapons actually
behaved as predicted and tests of nuclear weapons since Hiroshima and Nagasaki have been necessarily very imperfect
laboratory exercises and not practical demonstrations.
Waiting to see what nuclear weapons will do on the day
presents an unanswerable argument for postponing that day.

This conclusion will fail to satisfy many people. A nuclear
peace secured by deadly fear is no failsafe: it is too novel to
be entirely credible and too amoral to be entirely acceptable.
And even if mutual nuclear deterrence works in practice,
that adventitious benefit does not lessen the moral enormity
of a nuclear war: the weapons are one thing, a war another.
Attitudes are conditioned by the nature of war rather than
its likelihood.

IV

Throughout recorded time opinions about the morality of
war have differed. There is, however, little room for differences about the morality of war in the nuclear age. The
progress of war presents the churches with a challenge to
retrace their steps and disown the compromise which official
Christianity made with the Roman state in the fourth
century, an opportunity to denounce war unequivocally. For

much the greater part of their 2000-year history the major strands in Christianity have accepted war not merely as something hard to avoid but also as an activity justifiable and even meritorious in certain circumstances – morally acceptable as well as practically inevitable. Some strands, such as the Quaker, have maintained a more principled pacifism but even they have witnessed and permitted active belligerence by many of their members. This uneasy compromise, made because the church believed that the alliance between church and state was necessary for the survival of Christianity, developed over the centuries into militant support for secular causes with Christian linings (the crusades, for example) and later for antagonistic nationalisms which won the more or less enthusiastic backing of state churches; various devils from heresiarchs and infidels to Kaiser Bill and communist chiefs have facilitated this Christian approval for war which, in modern times, has lost almost all its initial justification and become an adjunct of state policies, not moral purpose. The churches have tried to preserve their self-respect and doctrinal integrity by dictating terms for the waging of wars, but this role of the superego has by now been exposed as an illusion and a fake since no government in the world – not even the most avowedly Christian – now alters its policies or its practices at clerical command. Two things have happened: first, the Christian compromise has become devalued; secondly, the evaporation of the churches' regulatory powers has raised the question of reverting to the primitive stance of maintaining that war is not to be regulated but to be condemned. The advent of the nuclear factor has precipitated such debate although it does not, logically and by itself, require the abandonment of the Just War doctrine by which the churches have set their course for nearly 2000 years. On the one hand nuclear weapons may be said to have raised war to such a level of unacceptability that it must be comprehensively rejected. On the other, it may be argued that nuclear weapons have simply made the calculation of the justness or unjustness of a war easier by removing from the calculation any war in which such weapons will or may be used – and leaving other wars to the arbitrament of old established rules. On this latter view the rejection of nuclear war is an application of the doctrine of Just War, an application of an old tradition to new circumstances, whereas the former view entails the radical step of altogether discarding that tradition.

The radical alternative is a hard one because it comes near to being an admission of guilt. It also raises one of those questions that have no answer: whether it is better to insist on how things ought to be or to start from where things are. The Christian compromise has rested on a valid view of the world as it is, with wars as part of the way of the world. Rejection of war, on the other hand, supposes a world changed, a world not as it is but as it ought to be. But this radicalism does not sit easily in church and becomes even more suspect when, outside church, it rubs shoulders with radicalisms of a different stripe. Anyone can see that the world could be a better place but most people are scared of schemes for making it so, and perhaps even more scared of some of the unpredictable consequences of embarking on such schemes. *In extremis* – in, for example, areas of frightful poverty and injustice in Latin America – Roman Catholic clergy have adopted radical attitudes and even radical theology but they are frowned on by the main body of their universal church, including the Pope himself. It is easier for those in comfort and in authority to face with stoicism the miseries of others than to endorse the risks of radical change, and churchmen pulled two ways on moral issues are the more easily dissuaded from the radical side when religious radicalism becomes entangled with social radicals, even perhaps communists. It is significant both that CND has had a Roman Catholic priest as its general secretary and that Monsignor Bruce Kent excites the deepest suspicion and alarm within clerical establishments. If this is a paradox, it is an enduring one.

9

Rules

The law's prime aim is to reduce the use of force to settle disputes or pursue vengeance. In this purpose international law is no different from national law. The law does not envisage the elimination of force: that is an utopian, not a lawyer's vision. No legal system comes anywhere near to being able to bring about the elimination of force, which remains endemic and common even in the best ordered and most peaceful societies; but the law regulates its use and disallows it in stated circumstances and the lawyer asserts that an imperfect legal system is better than a system based on anything other than law, which assertion commands considerable consent. As a matter of practical convenience and common sense an individual is content to renounce the use of force, if not completely, yet extensively: he will, for example, cling to his right to use force to defend himself and his family and to prevent the theft of his goods but he will accept a prohibition on the use of force to recover these goods once they have been stolen: the victim of a theft must turn to the police and the courts to get his stolen property back.

This system does not work particularly well. The greater part of stolen property is never recovered by the police for its owners, but nevertheless there is no serious movement to abolish the system and revert to the 'law' of the jungle. Victims demand that the system be improved, not that it be abrogated so that they may take the 'law' into their own hands. (Note that the use of the word 'law' in both these cases is a misuse since the law of the jungle is the absence of law and taking the law into one's own hands means taking action in defiance of law.)

International legal systems are even less effective than domestic or national ones. Also they operate more obviously against the interests of the more powerful members of the society which they seek to regulate. Domestic systems have the great strength of providing a powerful class with something it wants – the certainty and comparative stability without which the civilian bourgeoisie, which began to displace the warrior class in western Europe in the later Middle Ages, cannot feel secure of life or limb or property, or secure in the conduct of its business. As this class developed into a ruling class it saw lawyers and law as allies, particularly in the development of the law of contract; and in return for these benefits of settled law – habitually observed and fairly often enforced – the new men of the western world, like their counterparts of the ancient Roman republic, were prepared to support an imperfect legal system rather than rely on currying the whimsical favour of lords and kings.

The attempt of the last few centuries to extend the rule of law to international affairs has limped. The main reason for this debility is not, as commonly alleged, the absence of a law-making body. The sources of international law are well attested* and its substance is no more imprecise than that of other branches of law. But when it comes to the abnegation of the use of force international law lacks the appeal which national systems possess in the eyes of influential persons. Whereas the extension of the rule of law within the state conferred benefits which outweighed the restraints, with international law the reverse is true, the shackles of law are more obtrusive than the benefits and so those members of the international society with the capacity to use force – the stronger states – are not prepared to renounce it. The state is still more warrior than bourgeois, in spite of the growth

* These sources are, first, treaties; secondly, custom, roughly the equivalent of natural law or common law in that it appeals to a body of mixed practice and belief; and thirdly, judicial decision. Peace treaties may be distinguished from other treaties when it is argued that they are imposed, not freely contracted, and so to some degree invalid: an unsettling but not illogical doctrine.

of international trade and finance. Even when states pledge themselves to peaceful ways of settling their disputes, they have mental reservations that national interests override international obligations and may justify national statesmen in preferring, in circumstances to be judged by themselves, the ambiguities of the former to the letter of the latter.

There are large areas of international law which have nothing to do with the matter of peace and war – for example, rules concerning the validity in one country of a divorce obtained in another. International law impinges upon the rights and duties of individuals as well as those of states, and even in the latter area international law covers much that is irrelevant to keeping the peace. The law relating to peace, now pre-eminently embodied in the UN Charter, is a comparatively compact segment. But before examining the state to which that law has now come there are two important preliminaries to be considered. The law relating to peace and war is not so entirely co-extensive with the law relating to states, as at first sight appears; and, secondly, the regulation of states' rights and duties on the basis of the legal sovereignty of the state is not logically the only approach to the ordering of international affairs.

For centuries it has been recognised that states make wars and it is hardly possible to write a book such as this one without repeatedly stating that they do. Yet the statement, if not wholly untrue, is a dangerous oversimplifaction. A state is an abstraction and strictly speaking it does nothing. Modern theorists of international relations have accentuated the confusion by referring in their jargon to states as 'actors' in international affairs. But the state is more an instrument than an actor and to call it an actor is to depreciate the rule, and therefore the responsibility, of the individual statesman or the committee of statesmen who activate the state.

The state is legally a person (*persona*), like a corporation. This is a legal fiction, sound and useful, but again it misleads in so far as it attributes to the state an automotive capacity such as belongs only to an individual or group of individuals. The war-making propensity of the state, which has fostered the attempt to bring the state under the rule of law, has obscured the need to apply the rule of law to real persons as well as fictive legal persons. So far as it goes the rule of law has prevented some wars, although it is impossible to be precise about how many. Nevertheless wars still occur, from which state of affairs two conclusions inescapably emerge: the effort to extend the rule of law is worthwhile and not to be abandoned or hampered, but likewise it is not enough. Extension means devising more stringent rules about the initiation and conduct of war, enforcing those rules, and also the application of the law to statesmen so that they may be held responsible for the state's infringements of the law.

The accountability of individuals for acts of state is not a popular subject with statesmen, nor has their reluctance to accept responsibility, legal or moral, been powerfully challenged either by popular opinion or by the law, both of which have been inclined to treat leading public figures indulgently. Only the historian, ruminating after the event, has habitually tried to fix upon statesmen a degree of responsibility for international events, good or bad. Thucydides, without going to the lengths of identifying the statesman with the state, made clear to his readers that much of what happened in the Peloponnesian wars arose out of the culpable mistakes of individuals. His followers in the practice of history over the next two thousand years have not been slow to portray individual statesmen as villains, but the law has been much slower to call them culprits. However, the prosecutors in the trials of major war criminals held at Nuremberg and Tokyo after the second World War set out to pin on individuals accountability for crimes not normally brought home to top people and likewise to extend the area of what, even in wartime, is criminal.

By their very nature trials focus on individuals – on their own actions and their responsibility for those actions. Within this general framework the Nuremberg and Tokyo trials had two main aims: to apply the known laws of war, and to test the scope of law in related areas by advancing relatively untested arguments and getting a court to consider and pronounce upon them. Since there was in existence no standing court competent to do these things, such a court had to be established. This was done by treaty – an unusual but not unprecedented procedure. It was a civil court, not a court martial, with the important consequence that civil rules and procedures were adopted, including the delivery at the

end of the trial of judgments explaining the court's reasoning
on the legal issues and its verdicts on the individual defendants. The Tokyo trial, while in various respects different
from that at Nuremberg, had also these main features.

The Nuremberg indictment embraced familiar and less
familiar aspects of law. War crimes had been brought before
courts for centuries and there was nothing new about the
idea of war crimes or a war crimes trial. In this department
Nuremberg broke no new ground. But the indictment did
not confine itself to this kind of charge. In addition to war
crimes it covered two other branches of law – crimes against
peace and crimes against humanity. Both were obscurer than
war crimes and, on that account alone, proper matter to be
brought before a tribunal. The former (which were included
after a tussle in which the Americans prevailed over more
conservative Russian and French doubts) involved the allegation that the coming of war was not just bad luck or even
bad management but flowed, in part at least, from guilt
which was judicially cognisable as a crime against peace. The
tribunal accepted after much argument the existence in law
of such a crime but applied it very cautiously to the issues
and persons before it. Crimes against humanity – the third
of the Nuremberg categories – were narrowly defined. To
come within the court's jurisdiction these crimes had to have
been committed during World War II and 'in connection
with' some other crime alleged in the indictment. The
charges under this heading were aimed at criminal acts
perpetrated against Germans, e.g. in concentration camps.
They too were dealt with by the court circumspectly but, as
with crimes against peace, the upshot was to establish
through judicial process that crimes of this kind were known
to the law and were justiciable before an international
tribunal. Thus international law was, if not greatly extended,
at least shown to be wider in scope than many had supposed
and a little more effective in practice.

Such advances have a price. The Nuremberg trial incurred
criticism which has continued against it. The main charge is
that it was a trial of the vanquished by the victors and so
contrary to natural justice. That it was a trial of vanquished
by their victors is indisputable, but it does not follow that
the actual proceedings or the verdicts were vicious. The trial

took the form it did because there was a choice between a trial of that kind or none; neutrals were unwilling to take on the responsibility and there was in existence no international standing tribunal with the necessary competence (the Permanent Court at the Hague had no criminal jurisdiction). That the defendants had an unfair trial or sustained unfair condemnation can hardly be maintained by anybody who was present at the trials or who has mastered the subject-matter. That charges could not be laid against any but the defeated was deplorable but explained not only by the temper of the times but again by the non-existence of a standing criminal tribunal.

The Nuremberg and Tokyo trials did enforce international law and clarify it, a matter which – besides punishment – is a principal function of any judiciary. But judicial review is not a promising way to extend the rule of law in international affairs since such trials occur only in the context of war and must in the continuing absence of standing international judicial machinery be rare. Efforts to create such machinery have been predictably abortive since sovereign states, which alone may create international courts, are exceedingly reluctant to do so. That national courts are no adequate substitute was demonstrated by the one major war crimes trial to be initiated since 1945 – that of Lieutenant John Calley for crimes committed at My Lai – which ended with a ludicrously mild sentence and without any attempt to pursue any but the lowest ranking officer involved.

II

The second important general topic – no less important than the accountability of individuals – is the assumption made by international law that the proper basis for the relations between states is their legal sovereignty. It follows from this assumption that one state may intervene in the affairs of another either not at all or only in the most restricted circumstances: forcible intervention is superlatively wrongful. This doctrine has a crucial political consequence: peace between states is paramount.

Yet the argument and its consequence are questionable. Should injustice and inhumanity be protected by frontiers? Is there no right or obligation to intervene in a state where terrible things are being done to human beings, to intervene even by war? Lawyers and others have argued about the so-called right of humanitarian intervention. At present this right is distinctly unfashionable with lawyers and statesmen although Tanzania's invasion of Uganda to put an end to Idi Amin's barbarous tyranny raised embarrassing doubts about the adequacy of a doctrine which said that President Nyerere should not have done it. Although his legal pretext was feeble, his action was not widely condemned. In practice, any such intervention against a major state (or perhaps one of its protectorates) is unthinkable because the risk of a serious war inhibits it.

The present tendency is to cope with this dilemma by a stringent limitation on the right of intervention. An operation to rescue nationals, whether successful like Israel's at Entebbe in 1976 or unsuccessful like President Carter's in Iran in 1980, is held to be permissible. Whether co-religionists (the Falashas, for instance) may be equated for this purpose with nationals is more dubious, although the protection of Christians was commonly given as an excuse for European intervention in Ottoman affairs in the nineteenth century. But whoever may be covered by this rule, they must be in evident danger; President Reagan's pretence that Americans in Grenada were in danger could not pass muster as a pretext for his invasion of that island in 1983. Motive counts too. A rescue operation designed as cover for the overthrow of a foreign government is illegal and it is even arguable that a rescue which cannot succeed without overthrowing a government is necessarily illegal, from which it would appear that no rescue is permissible unless those to be rescued are few. In other words, where there is a conflict between respecting the legality of a government and rescuing victims of oppression the former prevails.

But the gravest argument against a wider right of humanitarian intervention is that the exercise of such a right is too often a cloak for the pursuit of national interests. Such a right is by its nature imprecise, and its exercise therefore suspect and subject only to *post hoc* justification. It places in the hands of the powerful an instrument which they cannot be trusted to use solely for the purposes for which it is given.

There is a further but equally flawed argument against basing international order on the legal concept of sovereignty and its corollary, non-intervention: namely the appeal to self-determination. Self-determination proclaims the right of a people to determine its own form of government and the right therefore to secede from a state in which it constitutes a distinct people: what constitutes a distinct people is in almost every case disputed but the right is held to subsist even though there may be disagreement in a particular case about who are its beneficiaries. If a people is seeking to assert its right against opposition, or if the right is patently violated, may outsiders intervene to uphold the right? Such action must on occasion entail, or at least risk, war and cannot in such a case be undertaken unless peace has a lower priority than self-determination.

Both Superpowers have invoked democracy or the right to self-determination as a pretext for the use of force against a sovereign state. The Brezhnev Doctrine, which was enunciated at the time of the Soviet invasion of Czechoslovakia in 1968 and is a rationalisation of the case for making war, asserts the right of the Soviet Union to use force to maintain in neighbouring states what it calls socialism and democracy. President Reagan, a decade later, went even further when he claimed a duty upon the United States to intervene in Central America not merely to preserve democracy but to instal it: his intervention included arming rebels (the Contras) against the established government of a sovereign state, Nicaragua, and mining its coastline. The Thatcher government in Great Britain went almost all the way in support of Reagan's contentions and actions, although in the case of Grenada it betrayed some irritation at receiving no prior intimation of the armed invasion of a sovereign member of the Commonwealth.

These arguments, Russian and American, are vicious because of their casuistry. In Czechoslovakia the Russians were pursuing their own interests which had nothing to do with socialism or democracy. In Nicaragua the Americans were looking for excuses to overthrow a government which they much disliked and vaguely feared. But even if Moscow and Washington had been honest their espousal of a political nostrum like self-determination in place of the legal concept of sovereignty as the organising principle of an international system is mistaken. First, it undermines the system in existence, which has been developing for centuries and which, however imperfect, has a history and a rationale permitting further development. Secondly, a political criterion like self-determination is too vague and too open to abuse to underpin an international system or secure adequate consent for a system so constituted: it is not an acceptable alternative to law. And, finally, invoking the principles of self-determination or democracy or socialism – or whatever – legitimises the use of force, increases the occasions for war and, while appearing to adapt to modern times the doctrines of Just War, ignores the conditions governing Just War both as to its initiation and its conduct. While posing as a democratic defence of peoples, it is in effect an open licence to attack states.★

★ A related problem may be mentioned. A state may, in some circumstances, use force in support of the government of another state. But it may not do so if that government has been overthrown and a successor is effectively in control. There is no right to intervene to restore a fallen government. Further: one government may legitimately respond to an invitation from another government to intervene. But the invitation must be genuine and not a *post hoc* fabrication or excuse. The allegation that Soviet forces entered Hungary in 1956 and Afghanistan in 1979 by unforced invitation and because of such an invitation is as nonsensical as Reagan's plea that he invaded Grenada in order to save American lives there.

III

There is no getting away from the sovereign state. A workable international order must accept the concept of sovereignty and be built round it. But, as internationalists have been saying for generations, the state may be curbed in the exercise of its sovereignty. Hence their designs for international organisations in which states voluntarily and contractually renounce some of their powers and, in the latest of these organisations – the UN – renounce even the right to make war (except in self-defence).

This abnegation is the most significant, indeed startling, event in the gradual erosion of the unfettered sovereignty of the state. Article 2 of the UN Charter, which transfers the right to make war from the state to the international body, is no more effective at present than was *habeas corpus* during the Wars of the Roses, but the very fact of its existence and its acceptance by virtually all the states in the world is an extraordinary innovation which can never be entirely erased. The idea of securing peace through international organisation continues fitfully to flourish even though the UN's machinery for resolving disputes without war and for international law enforcement has been stultified by the Cold War and undermined by both Superpowers.

This is curious. If ever an institution was decried and discredited it was the League of Nations in the thirties. Yet in 1945 the UN was created in the image of the League with essentially the same constitution, aims and hopes, chief among these the prevention of wars. The UN's founders thereby proclaimed their belief that the League had been on the right lines and its defects could be cured. They were right. But they could not guard against the new pitfalls which were to afflict the UN.

The League's chief defect, so it was believed, was that it lacked 'teeth' – in other words, executive capacity. This was a two-pronged judgement implying one or both of two things: that the League's constitution (the Covenant) did not go far enough in vesting powers in the international body alongside or instead of national states, and/or that the League's leading mentors did not together command the power to shoulder the responsibilities laid upon them by the Covenant. Both conclusions were broadly true, remediable and tackled by the UN's founders.

The Covenant of the League did not outlaw war. It provided alternative mechanisms for settling disputes and required members to use these mechanisms before going to war. But war remained a legitimate exercise of state power if the mechanisms were used to no avail; and the attempt by the Geneva Protocol of 1924 to introduce compulsory arbitration of disputes when the mechanisms failed was rejected by the British and Dominion governments and so collapsed. In consequence the League – in relation to war and peace – was never more than an international convenience which had to be used so far as it went but did not forbid an ultimate resort to war. Article 2 of the UN Charter drastically reversed this situation.

The League's second famous weakness was also eliminated. The League was essentially an association of European powers. The headquarters were in Europe, its successive secretaries-general were Europeans and its most conspicuous and powerful members were Great Britain and France. These two were worldwide powers but they were worldwide powers which were losing their capacity to function as such, and this incapacity was the principal factor in the League's most spectacular failure, the Ethiopian crisis of 1935 – a crisis in Africa which fell upon European governments and was significantly conditioned by Asian and Pacific considerations. If the League system was to be upheld it was incumbent on Great Britain and France in particular to take the lead against Italy, the aggressor in Ethiopia. Neither the British nor the French were afraid of Italy. But they were anxious not to offend Mussolini and so drive him into alliance with Hitler and, for the British cabinet, the main argument against a tussle with Italy was provided by Japan. The Admiralty persistently impressed on the cabinet the Royal Navy's inability to become involved in a European conflict and at the same time honour its obligations to defend the Pacific

Dominions, pledges only recently and publicly reaffirmed. Great Britain's world power was by this date militating against firm action because its multiple obligations all over the world (including its obligations under the Covenant) exceeded or at least gravely strained its capacities. The cabinet feared that an embroilment in the Mediterranean, even if unlikely seriously to damage the Mediterranean fleet, might lure Japan into attacking Great Britain's valuable possessions, profitable investments and high prestige in South East Asia. Forced to choose, the British government recoiled from its obligations under the Covenant, carrying France not unwillingly with it, and since the power of the League was the power of these two members the League was rendered irrelevant. But in the UN this imbalance between powers and responsibilities was cured by the membership of the American, and to some extent the Soviet, Superpowers. The new body had, from its inception, a membership with a truly worldwide reach.

But it had other problems. In order to live up to the Charter's furthest aspirations the members – or at least the dominant members – had to act together. The Cold War dashed that hope. The mutual antagonism of the Super-powers destroyed that whole section of the Charter which was designed to buttress the bold radicalism of article 2. Since the founders of the UN did not believe that force could be eliminated from international affairs, they posited forcible international action in place of national action and proposed to equip the UN with an international military staff and an international military force. These have never come into existence. (*Ad hoc* UN peacekeeping forces, scratched toge-ther in a crisis and deployed on many occasions all over the world, are quite different. They are forbidden to use force except in self-defence and they cannot be despatched without the consent of the government of the country to which they are going.)

On top of the crushing blow inflicted on the UN by the Cold War mentality of its leading members – a blow from which it can hardly recover without a deep change in Super-power relations – the UN system has experienced a further and paradoxical setback. Whereas its worldwide reach is theoretically secured by the membership of world powers, its worldwide membership has weakened its overriding dedication to peace.

The UN membership, unlike the League's, is truly universal but this gain has its price. The mere increase in the number of members has introduced a cumbrousness which an organisation struggling to demonstrate its effectiveness can ill afford. The sense of community, which is essential to the idea of a functioning international system, is gravely eroded. Internationalists have supposed a community of interests among sovereign states which promotes co-operation and a community of tradition which lubricates it, and they have envisaged a concert of like-minded states willing and capable of reproducing at the international level the legal forms and political habits of the state itself (which, although commonly called a nation state, is more often than not a multi-nation hybrid). But the decolonisation of the 1960s and 1970s brought to the United Nations scores of new states with differing traditions, differing aims and differing priorities. Having only just attained statehood they are not sympathetic to schemes for shackling the power and the rights of the state; and although it would be libellous to decry their devotion to peace it is nonetheless true that peace is not automatically the first concern of governments whose peoples live in frightful poverty: the prime obligation of such governments is to make life a little better materially for their people, to engage therefore in sparring matches with the richer countries. Starvation seems even more ghastly, and is certainly more imminent, than war. So the conflict between rich and poor – the North/South conflict as opposed to the East/West conflict, a duel over the economic order rather than armaments – complicates international affairs and distracts the international society from the simple imperative of keeping the peace. This situation will not change for many a day.

Simultaneously the tension between national interests (self-evaluated) and international obligations persists and the primacy of war-avoidance, which seemed overwhelming in the shadow of the Second World War, has become less so with the prosecution of the Cold War. Americans and Russians, looking back in 1945 at the World War, were resolved that nothing like it must happen again. Americans and Russians involved in their current war are more concerned with how to conduct it. The Brezhnev doctrine, already cited, gives priority to the maintenance of Soviet-style socialism over the avoidance of war and so sanctified the overthrow of Dubcek by armed invasion. President Reagan, exalting the American mission to give democracy to the politically deprived, engages in wars by despatching not merely arms (many states make friends and money that way) but also military staffs and military contingents to help overthrow established governments; and in pursuing this aim he not only asserts that an established government is not immune unless it is in his eyes good, but also tries to bend the UN Charter to his purposes.

Article 51 of the Charter preserves the state's right to individual or collective self-defence.* It does so subject to conditions: the right endures only until the Security Council takes necessary measures to maintain international peace; the state acting in self-defence must immediately report its actions to the Security Council; and that state must not in any way affect the Security Council's authority or its responsibility to maintain or restore peace. The right of self-defence is therefore both retained by the Charter and circumscribed. But neither in the Charter nor elsewhere is it defined. Some acts are clearly self-defensive, others clearly not; and there is a grey area when argument flourishes unresolvable. Those who drafted the Charter appear to have had in mind a direct physical attack across a common border and immediate riposte by the attacked: the situation with which nation states are most familiar. At some undefined point a less immediate riposte ceases to be self-defence and becomes retaliation and so is not covered by Article 51 and, if force is used, constitutes an infringement of the Charter. Retaliation is probably, but not certainly, the correct appraisal of the British expedition to recover the Falkland islands. The Argentine *coup de main* was a clear breach of the Charter but

* Article 51 was a last-minute addition to the Charter in response to cries of alarm from members of existing international bodies (the Arab League, the OAS) who feared that, without an article of this kind, their own regional rules would be overruled. It has been invoked to justify India's invasion of Bangladesh and Tanzania's of Uganda as well as the American bombing of Tripoli and Benghazi.

it did not automatically validate the British response. A
British force on the islands would unquestionably have been
entitled to shoot back at the invaders in self-defence but the
despatch of an armada from England to recover the stolen
possessions was at best a dubious recourse to self-defence.
Even the prompt British declaration of an intention to use
force if necessary cannot be held to justify the expedition if
it was illegal *ab initio*.

The Reagan administration has gone further. Seizing on
the words 'collective self-defence' in Article 51 the President
has argued that the United States may take part in hostilities
between two other states by dubbing one an ally and the
other an aggressor against that ally. On this basis the United
States could encourage a friendly state to engage in war
with another whose government the United States wishes to
overthrow and then join in and overthrow it – an unlikely
reading of the Charter. The truth is more restrained. 'Collective self-defence' is a vague phrase and strictly speaking a
contradiction unless two or more states are attacked simultaneously (in which case the issue does not arise). Its use in
Article 51 permits UN members which already have a
relevant treaty with each other to honour that treaty when
one of them is attacked. But in order to meet the case
envisaged by Article 51 there has to be a pre-existing defence
treaty and there has to be an armed attack, not merely vilific-
ation or subversion.

Between the wars Great Britain and France let down the
League and sabotaged it but they did so largely because they
lacked the capacity to do otherwise. Half a century on the
Superpowers of the second half of the century have flouted
and belittled the UN not because of any lack of power but
because they do not set a high value upon it. Their scepticism
has been so reinforced by the antagonism generated by Cold
War and simplistic ideologies that they have derogated from
internationalism and weakened the rule of law instead of
trying to champion them.

Yet the UN is still the best international system available
and the extension of law to international affairs is the only
effective way to lessen the war-making of states. Nuclear
terror and the balance of terror may inhibit wars between
states which possess great nuclear armouries and some

political sophistication – in effect, wars between the Super-powers. But these wars are only a part of the problem and, in terms of the number of situations capable of producing war, a very small part.

The UN furthermore has shown an inventiveness in controlling wars which no state or national statesman has approached. It has created for itself a role in stopping wars and has done this pragmatically by taking action in a crisis and developing the function which was then thrust upon it. The peace-keeping role of the UN, of which there is no mention in the Charter, began with the Suez war of 1956 when the Anglo-French-Israeli attack on Egypt miscarried, the aggressors had to be extricated for their own good and without too much loss of face, and the job was handed without any notice to the UN which had never before under-taken any operation of this kind. Since that haphazard begin-ning peace-keeping by composite UN forces has become sophisticated, flexible and not uncommon, freezing torrid situations and putting into reverse the accelerating tempo of tit-for-tat leading to war. The limitations of the UN are obvious but statesmen who bustle to New York to read the UN lessons in behaviour and to publicise its shortcomings weaken an organisation which they ought to be doing all in their power to strengthen.*

---

* The most blatant attempt to sidetrack the UN proved this point. When the United States, obedient to Israeli antagonism to UN forces, put a multi- but non-UN force into Beirut to keep the peace, this force did the opposite; it exacerbated local conflicts, contributed to them by delivering a naval bombardment and, after a humiliating display of incoherence and inexperience, had to be removed.

IV

Various kinds of belligerence fit uneasily into an international state system. With the growth of the power of the state it has become common to label as war only those kinds of organised violence which are conducted by a state. Belligerence by non-states is denied the name of war and called something else. Civil wars and guerilla warfare have achieved recognition as sub-species of war; anti-colonial liberation movements attained a degree of respectability in some quarters, although no precise legal status; but there remain further kinds of belligerence, commonly disparaged as terrorism. This is a word to beware of. It has become a term of abuse, used to excite prejudice and fuel unthinking reactions – which is all the more deplorable since terrorism does exist and has to be countered.

Terrorism entails killing people for a political end. It is distinct from murder for vengeance or private gain. It is used by the weak against the strong and by the strong against the weak. States use terror and even create constitutionally special bodies licensed to kill unlawfully (the KGB and the CIA being only two among many such agencies) but states cannot sensibly be called terrorist since their use of terror is a minor and ancillary part of their activities. A terrorist organisation is best defined as one which uses killing as a principal instrument – a definition which in practice excludes all or most states at most times but does not exclude them by definition.

The use of violence by non-states may be confined to a particular state or it may be international in the sense of operating from one state on a number of others. The domestic variety, which is distinguished from other riotous crime by its political ends, is usually radical but sometimes ethnic. Western Europe and Latin America have provided the outstanding examples in recent years. Its principal characteristics are a fervour which overrides common norms of humanity and legality, the smallness of the groups using it and their failure to achieve their aims. Minorities opposed to the government of the states in which they live – Basques in Spain, Tamils in Sri Lanka, Kurds in Iraq or Turkey or Iran – use violence to get autonomy or simply better treatment; sometimes they demand secession (Biafra, the Polisario). Mostly they are on their own and affect international affairs only if their domestic grievances provide opportunities for international meddling (of which more below). Social revolutionaries, although they direct their violence against their own government, are the more likely to have foreign contacts, sympathisers and support. The leaders of the West German *Rote Armee Faktion*, the Italian *Brigate Rosse* and similar groups got to know each other, shared their experiences and were keen to help each other. So are revolutionary groups in Latin America. In practice their co-operation amounts to little but their confraternity (particularly that of left-wing groups which get help from the Soviet Union) enables their enemies to portray them as an international conspiracy. In western Europe their activities have amounted to insurrection which failed to reach the level of civil war; in Latin America to insurrection which reached that level and then – except in Nicaragua – failed.

An international dimension is more evidently added to belligerence of this kind when the belligerent group is not attacking its own government, either because it has none or because its enemies are dispersed abroad. These groups fall into two, not easily distinguished categories. Some are little more than criminal gangs and can only be treated as such, while others are more substantial, more strictly organised and – at least in their own eyes – potential states equipped with some of the apparatus of statehood and claiming recognition as states (the PLO and the ANC being the clearest examples): to treat these as mere gangs is to fly in the face of fact.

The members of a gang which resorts to crimes such as murder or kidnapping do not cease to be criminal because they profess political aims or even if they justly claim to be the victims of political iniquity. The criminal activities of such gangs fall within the criminal law and have to be countered by the normal methods of criminal detection and pursuit. A part of their success is due to the weakness of the police, national or international, but that is a reason for improving police co-operation and does not justify indiscriminate retaliation or acts of war.

Before branding an organisation as terrorist two general factors have to be considered. First, an organisation may shift from the terrorist category to the non-terrorist or *vice versa*. It has to be judged by its actions at a given time and not by sticking a label on it. Secondly, those actions have to be judged in the context of surrounding circumstances. Trigger-happy violence is different from the violence born of despair: there are organisations whose members go out and shoot people because they have got into the habit of doing this and little else, and there are other organisations which resort to violence because they have no alternative except letting themselves be crushed by superior violence. Desperation goes at least some way towards justifying violence, even on occasion lethal violence: it raises a case which requires to be examined.

Warmaking by groups outside the regular forces of a state first became a problem in modern times with the activities of irregular opponents of invaders or occupiers of the national territory. These activities were a concomitant of the rise of nationalism. Napolean learned about them in Spain, where they got the name *guerilla* meaning little war or quasi-war, and in 1812–13 in Russia and Germany; and they played a part in both the World Wars of the twentieth century, in the first particularly in Belgium and in the second all over Europe and in South East Asia. Organised armed opposition to alien empires beset the Roman empire in its decline and, not so very differently, European empires in Africa in the present century. By the latter part of the nineteenth century a national war was widely considered to be a Just War and therefore legitimate, and in the twentieth century anti-colonial wars gained the same sympathy. Those who waged them were distinguished from civil warmakers. They had come therefore half way to being international as distinct from national figures and their wars were half way to being incorporated in international law. This was a dubious and untidy development which has been relegated to history by the success of liberation movements and the end of their wars.

But not quite. The ANC pledged to overturn white supremacy in South Africa; the PLO pledged to destroy the state of Israel; and the IRA pledged to evict the English from Ireland – all these organisations use some of the language of liberation and, whatever their language, engage themselves more or less effectively against the governments of sovereign states. And even if they were all to be crushed tomorrow – to become examples of those who took the sword only to perish by the sword – it is barely conceivable that there will never be another similar organisation without the resources and the sympathy to enable it to make war for a long time.

Since the Second World War the prospects for this type of warfare have improved. Technical developments have made all warfare more devastating; weapons are relatively easy to come by, even when they are not supplied by major powers for selfish political or financial reasons (larger states like to foster hostilities by third parties so that they themselves may remain in the background); and above all because it has had on occasion some sparkling successes (Israel, Algeria, Zimbabwe, for example). The facile notion that violence does not pay is a particularly silly apothegm. Post-World War II history begins with the conspicuously successful terrorist campaigns of Jewish organisations to drive the British and the Arabs out of Palestine by methods which have since been copied all over the world. The leaders of these Jewish groups achieved their immediate practical aims and so graduated from terrorism to statehood, becoming in the new Israel which they created by these means the leading statesmen in a widely recognised sovereign state. Their methods were in their own eyes justified by their cause and later terrorist organisations have not been slow to make the same claim. Each successive claim is inevitably met by the acquiescence of some and the abhorrence of others.★

Hitherto a sharp line has been drawn between every non-

★ The principal refinement of these tactics has been politcal kidnapping – of innocent individuals or, chiefly by hi-jacking aircraft, groups. The aims may be money, publicity or the release of imprisoned colleagues. Governments, remoter from emotional pressures than families or employers, habitually insist that they will not capitulate to blackmail but their refusal brings them perilously close to being accessories to the maltreatment or killing of hostages.

state body and the state, thus lumping together organisations like the PLO and ANC with minor and ephemeral gangs which, whether their aims be political or not, do not qualify as belligerents. The dividing line is in the wrong place; it should be re-drawn to distinguish between organisations which may and do accept the laws of war and gangs which could never be accorded belligerent status. The lines of demarcation already exist. As evolved during the nineteenth century they are: wearing a distinctive uniform or badge visible at a distance, accepting a recognised hierarchy of command, carrying arms openly, and accepting the laws and customs of war. (In the event of a sudden invasion the last two conditions were deemed to suffice. The last referred to a growing corpus of customary international law which was being embodied and expressed in international conventions concerning the treatment of the sick, the wounded, prisoners of war and civilians. Its main instruments in the nineteenth century were the Geneva Convention of 1864, the St Petersburg Declaration of 1868 and the Hague Conventions of 1899 and 1907.)

Initially the movement to encompass irregular forces in the laws of war had nothing to do with forces ranged against the state. On the contrary, the militias and volunteer corps referred in the Hague Convention were adjuncts, not adversaries, of regular armies and the intention was to extend to these legally ambiguous – and vaguely described – bodies the rights and obligations of regular armies which, in a crisis, the irregulars were expected to help against an invasion or enemy occupation.

This process has been considerably amplified, by for example the Geneva Conventions of 1949 which have themselves been extended by additional protocols (1977) and remain under continuous debate, academic and diplomatic. The Conventions of 1949, with their express reference to the UN Universal Declaration of Human Rights, attest the humanitarian impulse behind what is a gradual conversion of the laws of war into laws of armed conflict. The scope of positive law remains predominantly those irregular forces which are adjuncts of regular forces but there has also been a tendency to go further and embrace within the law forces conducting operations of war outside and beyond the strict category of inter-state wars.

The principal objects of these conventions are civilians, prisoners of war and the wounded – classes of people who may to some degree be spared or rescued from the horrors of war by insisting that they have rights and by providing special services to help them. And what may be done for such persons in a war between states may also be done for them in a war between a state and its non-state adversaries. Simply to dub the latter terrorists is no help to their victims, nor does it help to put a stop to the warfare.

A special variety of terrorism has been labelled international terrorism. Like plain terrorism, this term is an emotive political slogan to be eschewed by serious people; but, again like plain terrorism, it contains a hard morsel of disagreeable fact. It has two aspects. First, it implies that certain manifestations of terrorism are internationally inspired and aided, more precisely that they are inspired and aided by the Soviet Union and are part of a communist conspiracy to dominate the world. Although the Soviet Union uses all manner of nasty tricks at diverse times and places, such a conspiracy is nonsense and international terrorism in this sense does not exist, even in the minds of many of those who find it useful to proclaim that it does. Even within the smaller compass of Europe there is little internationalism about violent protest movements. The camaraderie between French and German and Italian militants in the sixties amounted to little more than an awareness of shared indignation, while South African claims that black governments and liberation movements dance to a Soviet tune is moonshine.

The second, more restricted and more real use of the term international terrorism connotes aid to a militant body in one country by the government of another. Much of this aid, probably most of it, is financial, although some of it is directly or indirectly devoted to the provision of arms.

Virtually all governments with money to spare spend some of it in foreign countries in ways that those countries do not like. This kind of interference is not in itself illegal, but it becomes illegal when its aims are illegal. This is the case, either if the giver's aims are themselves illegal, or if the recipient's use of the aid is predictably illegal. It is, for example, illegal for a state to try to overthrow the established government of another state, and transmitting or providing funds for such a purpose is an illegal act. It is also illegal to subsidise crime, so that the sending of money to an organisation addicted to murder or other forms of illicit violence is *a priori* illegal. In sum, it is not necessary to cross an international frontier in order to fall foul of the law. A military invasion, such as the Russian invasions of Czechoslovakia and Afghanistan or the Argentine seizure of the Falkland islands, is the most obvious infraction of international law but hostilities may be carried on in other ways and are no less illegal for that: for example, American actions designed to overthrow the government of Nicaragua by force of arms. But intervention of this kind cannot be described as terrorism, although its victims like to call it that. The charge of aiding and abetting terrorism at international level arises only when the intervention takes the form of subsidising or otherwise aiding a criminal organisation or gang as strictly defined above.

The organisations most frequently cited in this context are the PLO and the ANC. (The case of the IRA is different since its foreign funds come from American individuals and not from the American government. Libyan funds for the IRA, never prolific, seem to have dried up.) The PLO and the ANC are entitled to get what money they can from wherever they can, but if they are terrorist organisations, then their suppliers are acting illegally. The ANC argues that its cause (democracy) is just and that it has no alternative to violence in pursuing its aims because it is up against a regime which is equally violent and rejects any form of dialogue and all but trivial forms of compromise. This plea is a powerful one and, if it be allowed, then the ANC is not a terrorist organisation and there is no legal bar to helping it with money or otherwise. The case of the PLO is more complex. Palestinians have formed a number of organisations and it is not clear who controls which, or even which is responsible for a particular act of violence. It is hardly to be doubted that some Palestinian groups are so largely devoted to killing that they rank as terrorist, but it is far from clear that all of them belong to this category, as their enemies pretend. They get rich from various sources, mainly but not exclusively Arab and most ostentatiously – but not necessarily most effectively – from Libya. Where this aid is given in the knowledge that the recipients are no better than terrorists the aid is not only deplorable but also criminal. Libya under Gadafi's leadership has been notoriously indiscriminate in its patronage of violence, and Libyan aid to Palestinian groups devoted to violence (and to little else) has proliferated crime and death. More sinisterly, it so outraged President Reagan that he resolved to take military action in defiance of law and was overwhelmingly supported by the American people in this course. So between them Gadafi and Reagan downgraded the rule of law.

First, the hi-jacking of the holiday vessel *Achille Lauro* and the murder of one of its American passengers was followed by the clearly unlawful acts of forcing an Egyptian aircraft out of the sky and then trying to seize some of its passengers on Italian soil. Next, the attack by Palestinians on a club in West Berlin which killed two people was followed by massive American bombing of Tripoli and Benghazi. Described as reprisal for the incident in Berlin it was more correctly reprisal or retaliation for the general course of Libyan conduct and the half-hearted attempt to bring it within the UN Charter as permissible self-defence was so ludicrous as merely to add hypocrisy to illegality. The real reason for the attack – and its sufficient justification in the eyes of Reagan and his compatriots – was desire to do something stunning, despite the consequence that the legality or illegality of what was done had to be treated as secondary. The attack was not only a breach of the UN Charter and so of the United States' treaty obligations; it was also contrary to the laws of war as they existed for centuries before the Charter, since it clearly flouted the rule that the force used must not be disproportionate to the action giving rise to it and that innocent civilians must not be deliberately endangered.

Both the League and the UN have in the past tried to introduce some definition and control into this murky area of international affairs but drafts of anti-terrorist conventions, produced in 1937 and 1972, got no further than the drafting, and a more specific UN convention against the taking of

hostages, although adopted in 1979 in the wake of the seizure
of the American hostages in Iran, has been widely ignored.
The European Convention on the Suppression of Terrorism
(1976) is an attempt to discourage international political violence by facilitating the extradition of accused persons from
one country to another, and this restricted attack on the
problem has since been pursued by Britain in the special case
of members of the IRA who take refuge in the United
States.★

Thus far two principal conclusions emerge: that the use
of violence by non-states is, whether legitimate or not,
frequently successful; and that one way of limiting the consequent pain and damage is to draw a distinction between
belligerent organisations which are not strictly speaking
terrorist and those which are. The corollary of this second
conclusion is to recognise that the actions of the latter are a
matter for the police, national and international, while the
former may be brought under a degree of control by
applying to them the laws of armed conflict. To confuse the
two categories makes matters worse since, as the American
attack on Libya showed, the upshot is to add to the killing
of innocent persons, to bring the law into contempt and to
make no observable mark on the incidence of terrorism. If
the police cannot catch criminals, then the police need to be

★ The new Anglo-American extradition treaty is an example of special
cases making bad law. It erodes a sound general rule: namely, that extradition should not be available in political cases, since its application in
such instances too frequently leads to the torture and judicial murder of
the fugitives. The IRA's methods are akin to those of the PLO and the
ANC but its aims are different. Whereas the PLO aims to win statehood
by supplanting Israel and the ANC to win control of the existing state of
South Africa, the IRA aims to enlarge the Irish Republic by driving the
British out – means which are forbidden to the Republic itself. The
current troubles in Northern Ireland began over the refusal of the local
government to ensure the civil and political rights of the Roman Catholics.
This refusal has been used by the IRA to promote its campaign for the
union of the six counties with the Irish Republic instead of the United
Kingdom. British governments, with the mounting obtuseness born of
frustration, have helped the IRA, first, by failing to get the sub-govern-
ment in Belfast to put Roman Catholics on an equal footing with Protestants and, secondly, by resorting to a strident and negative rhetoric
which denounces the IRA's crimes but does nothing effective to save
anybody from them.

helped or reformed. Taking their job out of their hands does not catch criminals, any more than bombing Libyan cities discourages Palestinian terrorists, most of whom are controlled not from Libya but in the Middle East and can pursue their ends without Libyan money: making and planting bombs unfortunately costs little.

Between those who favour and those who reject a larger reliance on broadened international law lies a big question: How wide is the law to open its arms? The law confers rights and imposes obligations; it confers the rights in order to impose the obligations. But sceptics and conservatives are unpersuaded. They have more faith in containing violence by force than by law, and they believe that the legitimisation of the use of force (on whatever conditions) does more to increase it than to control it. They trust the law too little to be willing to extend its rule.

Governments distrust international law because they are national and not international and because they see in the international system more law than law enforcement. Since for political reasons they are unwilling to strengthen the enforcement, they are opposed to more law. They are therefore committed to crushing the feebler disturbers of the peace and restricted to fulminating against the stronger and more destructive bodies which continue their depredations and killings unconstrained. Governments recoil from the attempt to regulate the behaviour of these organisations because they prefer to hope for the unattainable solution of their extinction. They swat the flies and wring their hands over larger pests. So more people get killed.

The law's development has been charted by a shifting balance between conservative and expansionist forces. In the present age this perennial conflict has been bedevilled by two specially vexing problems: a clash of jurisprudential traditions and the active involvement of states in support of irregular belligerent organisations or gangs.

Hitherto international law has been a subject dominated by the European legal tradition (natural law and Roman law) and the evolution of the European state, but the universalis-ation of politics has forced the heirs of this tradition into contact with other heritages, some of which – notably those of China and Islam – are not only different but also intellectu-

ally and politically powerful.* On the legitimacy of violence
Muslims in particular have much to say and, more pertinently perhaps, have been forcing their views on the rest of
the world by their actions. In international affairs shi-ite
Muslims have been specially obtrusive. They belong to a
tradition in which suffering violence and inflicting it have
been common and fervid, and they inhabit a part of the
world whose sectarian conflicts are conjoined with acute
political and cultural clashes.

About one in ten Muslims are shi'ites. They separated
from the mainstream of Islam within a generation of the
death of the Prophet, thirteen hundred years ago. Their main
branch reveres the Prophet's son-in-law Ali, his two sons
Hassan and Hussain and their nine successors as the true
leaders of Islam who have been supplanted and persecuted
by the sunni establishment. The twelfth imam did not die
but disappeared and will re-appear – a fairly common notion
which, legends about the emperor Barbarossa show, is not
confined to religions. At the core of shi'ite Islam is a bottled
bitterness – Ali was murdered, Hassan probably murdered
and Hussain beheaded after losing a battle, and the memory
of these events is kept for ever fresh by annual celebrations
which tend to be as violent as they are mournful. Shi'ites
are acquainted with suffering and grief, with the call to
avenge suffering and the right to assail an usurping government. They have flourished more east than west of the
Euphrates and for nearly 500 years they have dominated
Iran. They rule in Bahrain, constitute (non-dominant)
majorities in Iraq and Lebanon, and form substantial minorities in Syria and Pakistan and among the Muslims of India.
Ayatollah Khomeini's seizure of power from the Pahlavi
dynasty in Iran emphasized the shi'ite nature of that country
and also alarmed Arab sunnis on two counts: first, that it
betokened a revival of Iranian interference in the Arab world
and, secondly, on account of shi'ite insistence that the state
and society should pay more attention to the clergy, and the
precepts of religion.

This second fear is the more pressing because shi'ite values
are not confined to shi'ites. Many sunni Muslims, while

---

* But there have been some cross-influences between Europe and Islam.

rejecting shi'ite beliefs and theories of government, concur in denouncing modern aberrations from islamic values and are equally prepared to use violence to make their point – as was shown, for example, by the murder of President Anwar Sadat in 1981 (an act undertaken as a pious duty and intended to trigger a radical revolution in Egypt with some similarities with the Iranian revolution of 1979). Sadat's assassin shared with the shi'ites in Iran and Lebanon a puritanism which becomes international when the modern vices which it hates, from capitalist materialism to topless bars, are blamed on the western world in general and the United States in particular. For many Muslims of all sects the word 'modern' means not so much progressive as alien: Sadat's offence was not merely his acceptance of an American alliance but also of an American way of life. In Lebanon this anti-Americanism becomes allied with shi'ite anti-jewishness. Shi'ites are in general more intolerant than sunnis (as the Bahais well know) and their religious hostility to Jews merges with their hostility to these friends and dependents of the United States and also with secular Palestinian opposition to the state of Israel. The explosiveness of this combination is sufficiently attested by the events of recent years which, given the reluctance of Arab states to go to war with Israel, takes the form of irregular war or terrorism. This belligerence in the Middle East, and its extension to foreign capitals where diplomats are murdered, is an alternative to regular war which acutely raises the question whether those who wage it – or which of them – should be brought within the laws of war. To do so is to give some recognition to their aspirations while insisting that these may be pursued by some means but not others; not to do so is to condemn but probably also to perpetuate all their methods without any inhibiting sanction.

What is in issue is the inadequacy of the definition of war. This entails no softness towards those who engage in war. On the contrary, the development of the law has been prompted, and is still prompted, by the wish to protect war's victims – civilians, the sick, the wounded and prisoners. There is neither need nor justification for including within the laws of war acts of violence by individuals or by groups which fail to pass the rigorous requirements for recognition as organised, disciplined and open political bodies. But bodies which do pass that test should, in the interests of their victims and in order to set limits to their violence, be recognised as belligerents whose members, if they transgress the laws of war, will be arraigned in accordance with those laws. Yet proposals by, for example, the Red Cross for revising the Geneva Conventions are frowned on by major powers and the refusal of the United States to sign additional protocols is used by the Soviet Union as an excuse to be equally obstructive. The law has its manifest weaknesses and loopholes but those who prefer rhetoric to law impede something which can be useful in favour of something which cannot and confine statesmen to the limited function of propagandists.

10

Action

Nuclear weapons have profoundly affected attitudes to some kinds of war and the UN Charter has radically altered the legality of war. But these are only preliminaries which may be or may not be translated into political action.

Those who form attitudes or frame laws are not men of action. Churchmen and lawyers live by rules – rules of conduct expressed in the one case in moral terms and in the other in legal terms: what a man ought to do and what he may do. Their business is to provide norms for others, not to cope themselves with the abnormal or the outrageous. They are better at going through the motions than going through the roof.

Politics, however, is a profession which demands above all skills in handling a crisis. If there were no call for critical decisions, there would be no need for political leaders: bureaucrats would do. So it is the business of politicians – or at least of those who assume the responsibility of directing national and international affairs – to act and to foresee the need for action. They are the successors of the kings whom the compiler of the Wisdom of Solomon adjured: 'You have the power and the sovereignty and a sore trial will fall upon you if you do not learn wisdom.'

But statesmen have only limited aptitude for this role. Many of them are disinclined to act because they come from decent settled backgrounds where action appears as disturbance, something to be undertaken only after thinking at least twice. This caution may on occasion be akin to wisdom; but the tendency to elevate caution into a prime feature of the equipment of a statesman is the beginning of disqualification for that title. Moreover, doing little or nothing for a long time may lead to doing explosively too much all of a sudden.

Statesmen nowadays seldom want war: it is perverse to pretend that they do. Yet they have two attributes which make them imperfect guardians of peace. They are up to their eyes in problems which become more taxing with every decade, so that with rare exceptions they give too little thought to the wider or longer view. They live in in-trays. They are even disposed to decry thinking about an uncertain future as unfit for practical persons and a distraction from the essential business of their kind – as though the future were not just round the corner. Secondly, they are perforce national leaders first and internationalists only second, if at all. At first sight this may seem not only inevitable but even proper in a world of nation states; but if the national interest includes (as it surely does) keeping the peace, then international good behaviour is a first charge on every statesman's time and thoughts. National interests and internationalism are not antithetical.

As a man of action in the international sphere the statesman therefore leaves something to be desired. He falls short because of the difficulty of reconciling his often disparate duties. Where then is more purposeful action to come from? Not, for reasons already given, from the sedentary professionals of the church and the law. Which leaves *vox populi* – popular pressures. Popular action may be designed as oppositional or supplementary; it may be an alternative to official action or a goad to it. The distinction is not clearcut but it is nevertheless crucial. Where popular action is directed against the state or its government that action will fail unless it can go the whole way to successful revolution (which is rarely the case and justifiable only in hopelessly awful situations). The more fruitful role of popular movements lies in putting stuffing into statesmen, not in knocking the stuffing out of them.

Peace is a resultant of two kinds of action: the actions of statesmen and the pressures upon them. Their action is decisive (or as decisive as any human action may be) but without outside pressures it is likely to be not enough. The pressures on statesmen include fear and other emotions but these are notoriously poor bases for judgement. They include also pressures from beyond the narrow circles of the political cosmos and officialdom – the voices of people at large who have less responsibility and often less knowledge but who have nevertheless given no less serious thought to public issues.

In many countries popular action of this kind is impossible. It is not allowed and is comprehensively repressed. Which is all the more reason why it should be encouraged wherever it is allowed. These are the countries which can make the most promising contribution to more peace and fewer wars.

Popular protest movements are an aspect of the symbiosis between government and people which is an accepted part of democracy. Protest is a form of participation in public affairs and is justified because the conduct of public affairs affects people: when it leads to war it kills them. It is therefore necessary to consider on the one hand the degree of participation available and, on the other, the limits upon it which may properly be imposed by the existence of, and in return for, democratic rights and procedures.

Parliamentary democracy, the commonest form, gives people considerable control over the nature of their government together with an assurance that they may exercise this right at prescribed and not infrequent intervals. Between these intervals people in a parliamentary democracy have only minor (and sometimes negligible) power indirectly exercised through elected representatives, varyingly amenable, who are under a threat of not being re-instated at the next election. All this is admirable but it does not go very far. It channels the popular right into a choice between political parties which may all seem unattractive to the voter or give scant attention to what he considers most important. So there is constant pressure for more democracy such as, for example, tighter or more frequent control over members of parliaments by their electors, or provision for a referendum which curtails the powers of the parliament by requiring that certain questions be referred to the whole electorate. These are constitutional devices, edging a parliamentary system towards more democracy. A protest movement, by contrast, accepts the system as it is but tries to influence the way it works from the outer edge. The people

– called by their detractors the crowd or, more demeaningly, the mob – clamour in the hope that authority will hear and may heed. Protest does not seek to undermine authority but does seek to influence it.

For the promoters and organisers of extra-parliamentary activity the principal question is how to make it effective. But that it not the only question, for there are limits to what is proper. The line between propriety and the impermissible may shift and is by its nature flexible as well as controversial, but two questions are inescapable. First, given a democratic society, must protesters always remain within democratically imposed rules of law? Secondly, is violence ever justifiable? These are two different questions since the law may be broken without violence

The rule of law, which has been a hallmark and test of civilised society from ancient times, displaces the rule of force and the rule of fear, and peace movements which seek to extend the rule of law from domestic to international affairs should be among the last to encourage or countenance breaches of that law. On the other hand it has to be conceded that the rule of law may be weakened by lawmakers as well as lawbreakers. Those who make and enforce bad laws, or laws unacceptable to the generality of citizens, bring the law into contempt and its maintenance into peril.

The law is what a section of the people make it at a given time, and since by common consent the law is changeable it follows that existing law can never be perfect. To maintain that imperfect laws must nevertheless be obeyed is to assert that an existing law has a more binding claim than a better law – that, in other words, obedience ranks higher than justice.

This is not a wholly acceptable proposition, still less a self-evident one. Some injustice is tolerable in the interests of maintaining a settled society but grave injustice may demand disobedience. The individual impelled by conscience or religion to break a law may be morally justified, at the price of accepting the penalties prescribed for that breach. The reason why a person breaking a law under the plea of conscience may not also claim exemption from the legal penalties attached to that breach is this: that moral justification for the breach derives from a moral code or system about which there is no universal assent, so that the lawbreaker's conscience is making an individual interpretation of that code or system and has no universal approbation for the breach. Because legality and morality are distinct, a moral claim confers no legal benefit and a morally justifiable breach of the law confers no exemption from the legal consequences of that breach.*

A law, besides being fallible in ideal terms, is also a construct. It is a set of rules laid down by a group of legislators in accordance with their own, necessarily partial, views of what is expedient, and occasionally in their own interests. Law is by its nature restrictive and its prohibitions may be, or be seen to be, discriminatingly repressive – an instrument of government fashioned by a ruling class (possibly subconsciously rather than malevolently) rather than an honest approximation to natural justice. A section of society which alleges that this is the case is making an allegation about the motives of the lawmakers and that allegation may be valid or false: it is not *a priori* false. In times of social strain the suspicion that the law is being made, or used, for sectional purposes becomes stronger, the more so if suspicions are inflamed by governmental secretiveness. A glaring example is the use by British governments of the ageing and ill conceived Official Secrets Act of 1912 (and specifically its section 2) which all parties have condemned at one time or another but which every successive government has retained less, it would seem, in defence of national security than as a convenience for fending off embarrassing questions and interuptions to bureaucratic routine.

An illegal act, such as is comprised in civil disobedience, is not *ipso facto* wrongful, although it may be. The attempt to equate illegality with immorality is casuistry. Morality and legality are sovereign but overlapping areas. Many actions are both, but no action is the one because it is the other.

The question of violence is a separate one. Violence is an extreme method of gaining an end – the end, in the case of demonstrators, often being to attract attention – or an

---

* This is the theme of the *Antigone* of Sophocles, who was a priest, and of many later dramas. Righteousness is no defence against lawful imprisonment or even execution.

incidental concomitant of something that started without a
firm intention to use violence. It is nearly always a breach
of the law. By its nature it requires much more stringent
justification than non-violent breaches of the law. But it is
logically impossible to say that it can never in any circumstances be morally justifiable. The morality or immorality
of an act of violence depends on a comparative assessment
of the harm done by the act and the harm which the act
plausibly sought to prevent. It would not have been immoral
to bomb Auschwitz. Or so it may be argued, and since the
argument is respectable it is impossible to lay down *a priori*
that all acts of violence are unarguably immoral. Violence is
an instrument of change and there is no logical or moral
basis for maintaining that there is no conceivable situation
which must be left unchanged if violence is the only way to
change it.

The dividing line between non-violence and violence is
less precise in practice than it is in language, particularly
when the issue is peace and war. Einstein, in a famous letter
to Freud in 1932, called himself a militant pacifist, thus
signifying a vigour in his pacifism which is barely consistent
with non-violence. Every protest movement, however corp-
oratively committed to non-violence, is likely to contain
members who are tempted into violence in varying
gradations from pushing and shoving to deliberate damage
to property and persons. If at one extreme there are those
who have foresworn every form of violence, at the other are
those who will stop at little in pursuit of their aims. The
latter are usually a minority, although opponents will seek
to portray them as more representative and numerous in
order to tar the movement as a whole with criminality.

The American civil rights movement has charted this
unstable relationship between violence and non-violence and
the tendency of the former, by a sort of Gresham's Law, to
displace the latter. The Campaign of Racial Equality
(CORE), founded in 1944, had a strong non-violent tinge
and a Gandhian resolve to use non-violence as a militant
technique. Martin Luther King, the movement's most
eminent figure, was a non-violent pacifist in the tradition of
Thoreau and Gandhi who, like the latter, organised and led
a mass campaign whose political purpose was grounded and

expressed in moral imperatives. The bus boycott in Montgomery, Alabama in 1955 – following the refusal of a black women to give up her white-only seat in a bus – was not only peaceful but also legal, as was demonstrated when the Supreme Court ruled segration in buses to be unconstitutional; and the Students Non-violent Co-ordinating Committee (SNCC), created in 1960, lived up to its name by holding up racism to shame through peaceful sit-ins in public places. Yet the more successful these activities, the more intensely did they raise the question why a good cause should respect the boundaries between non-violent and violent means and showed that in the absence of quick results non-violence would lose much of its appeal. King's violent death in 1968 helped to feed the anger and impatience which characterised such later movements as the Black Panthers (with their offshoot the Black Liberation Army).

There are people who enjoy violence, either venting bottled hatred or as a kind of fun, but most concerted violence has a calculated purpose. Thus the violence used by the British suffragettes was designed to accelerate the victory of their cause and it is at least unlikely that the politer and non-violent suffragists would have succeeded without the collateral methods of the suffragettes whose methods they fastidiously shunned. Violence has also proved effective on other occasions too numerous to require recall. The case against violence is not that it defeats itself or that it necessarily does more damage than good. The case against it is that it is intrinsically horrible, so that it ought to be avoided at almost any cost. Judgement can be made only case by case, usually after the event. The generalisations of moralists or politicians containing words like 'always' or 'never' are comfortable and convenient. But they are also intellectually disreputable. To say that violence is never justifiable in a democracy is – besides begging the question when is a democracy not a democracy – superficial silliness.

For their part governments cannot ignore breaches of the law, violent or non-violent, unless they be trivial. It is part of the business of government to maintain law. In doing so a government may act wisely or unwisely and protesters may bait it into heavy-handed overreaction. For this reason a government needs to beware of getting into the position of upholding laws which, besides being flouted by active protesters, are also deplored by a significant section of the passive majority who would otherwise steer clear of protesters. When governments insist on applying bad laws they are in one sense doing their job; but in another sense they are doing it badly and stupidly; and they bring discredit upon the rule of law. Protesters likewise discredit their own cause if their breaches of the law, or their challenge to the authority of government, exceed what seems fair and reasonable to the generality of uncommitted observers. And this in itself constitutes a further justification of popular protest by applying a popular brake to extravagant or malign protest.

If it be conceded that popular protest is on balance valuable, and if a protest movement manages to operate within broadly acceptable moral and legal limitations, a further question arises. How effective are such manifestations of popular opinion and popular wishes?

The statesman's first reaction is to mock such movements and he does not find it difficult to do so. A great deal of cheap abuse in moderately polite language is sprayed over campaigners such as the Greenham Common women who opposed the arrival in England of Cruise missiles. But campaigns of evident honesty and conviction, however unattractive some of their adherents may be said to be, are not easily disposed of by rhetoric alone. What damns them is failure. A popular movement will not get popular backing or acquire political weight unless it looks effective. It is easy to be a nuisance but essential to be something more.

Peace movements have not stopped wars or stopped governments from making or buying or using particular weapons. This generalisation may be challenged in relation to the Vietnam war which, although conducted with appalling new weapons and brought to an end by complex causes, cannot be described without some reference to the public outrage and outcry in the United States. This was a factor which the historian finds difficult to assess but cannot ignore; and its intrusion into the history books attests the growing significance of public protest. It is effective in two ways. Even though it fails, as CND has failed, in its immediate and proclaimed aims, it has other effects; and it discloses subliminal shifts in ideas, in this case ideas about the place of war in civilised societies.

Central to the activities of the revived CND of the eighties was the Stop Cruise movement. It failed in Great Britain, as did the cognate movement in West Germany, although elsewhere in Europe governments were jeopardised by the undertakings which they had given to the Nato Council or were forced by popular protest to go back on them. Cruise and (in West Germany) Pershing II missiles were duly installed and the protesters' main effort was therefore defeated. But CND and its allies succeeded in forcing their chosen issues into public prominence. In Great Britain pollsters were prompted to take soundings which showed significant majorities opposed to the introduction of Cruise (and also to the purchase of Trident missiles to replace Polaris in British nuclear submarines). Similar polls in other countries gave similar verdicts. The political impact of the debates and alignments thus provoked, although not precisely measurable, cannot be without consequence. A democratic government may scorn or denounce them, but it cannot ignore them, and without CND they would not even have come into the open.

Secondly, popular movements tell something of fundamental importance about the state of the nation. If human history is ultimately the history of ideas, then there is nothing more important for mankind than the processes of intellectual change. What makes ideas change is an exceptionally complicated subject (on which observations are offered in the next chapter) but even if we do not know how such changes come about, we may discern the signs and direction of change and need to be alert to do so. Statesmen and special interest groups are not well equipped to spot these changes since they are primarily and often exhaustingly concerned with the present and how to conduct themselves in the present in the light of the past: they are too preoccupied to have time over for anything else and are – with the rarest exceptions – professionally insensitive to changing moods. Popular movements, however, express these moods.

Throughout history wars have been regarded as inevitable, profitable (an obvious way to get what you covet) and healthy (they give scope to courage, loyalty, discipline:

virtues all). There have always been pacifists who have said
that war is wrong and intellectuals who have said that it is
senseless, but only in the present century has there been a
sizeable body of opinion which contradicts all the traditional
received ideas about war and maintains that we must and
can do without it. The existence of this protest discloses a
shift in opinion about war and, by disclosing it, augments
it.

Campaigns against nuclear weapons have marked a change
in the nature of popular anti-war protest. Between the two
World Wars popular indignation was aroused, typically, by
the Italian attack on Ethiopia at Walwal and by the bombing
of Guernica in Spain. Both were local incidents which
evoked horror by the slaughter of the innocent with modern
weapons: poison gas, air power. This was no way to make
war. Vietnam stirred similar feelings, magnified by the
crudity of American attitudes about killing goons: again, no
way to make war. But overlapping with the campaigns
against the war in Vietman as unjustifiably inhumane there
was the campaign against nuclear war anywhere – nuclear
war as such, regardless of any measure between ends and
means. Popular opinion moved from inveighing against
particular practices in particular instances to inveighing,
before the event, against nuclear war at any time and in any
cause.

The very fact that the protest can be couched in such
general and absolute terms shows that it is more moral than
pragmatic, more emotional than political. It is none the
worse for that, although more suspect thereby to pragmatists
and politicians. It disdains the rationalist argument that peace
may be kept by a balance of terror and queries the politicians'
claim to have the correct practical priorities. Its own practical
prescriptions are often unpractical in anything like foreseeable time: for example, the aims of European Nuclear
Disarmament (END) to remove all nuclear weapons from
the whole of Europe and establish an unified neutral Europe.
People who talk like that help the politicians whom they
assail – principally the new Anglo-American right and the
Kremlin's dinosaurs – to run rings round them for their
naivety. It is part of the stock in trade of politicians of
this stamp to suggest that peace movements are not only

infiltrated by subversives with ulterior motives (communists or CIA agents) but are in effect manipulated by these, while the movements compound this propaganda when they slide into moral self-righteousness or rage too furiously against politicians who are not so much villains as mediocrities.

Moralists have a hard time mustering support. They are saying that they are better, or have better standards or insights, than those whom they address and this is not a popular message. Neither statesmen nor populace like it. Furthermore, the moralist's denunciations have, by their nature, a broadly social as well as narrowly political range: they undermine the settled order. The Hebrew prophets provide a characteristic, if extreme, illustration. They denounced kings, priests and other mighty persons for their selfishness, corruption and blindness and lashed the people no less fiercely for their laxity and backsliding. They were better at inveighing than persuading. Thus Isaiah, counsellor to four kings, saw his advice taken by none of them and Amos, descending on Israel from neighbouring Judah, was deported in no time because the force of his message displeased. Yet they were right. Government and people were corrupted and myopic and would have done well to listen to the prophets even though they were demanding an unpalatable social and intellectual revolution. The prophets were the voice of protest.* They were unaccommodating, unattractive, unpractical, but they were right. Today the voice of protest comes from another quarter: it is *vox populi*. But its function, like that of the prophets, is to disentangle big issues from lesser ones and to belabour those whose business it is to deal with the maze of the latter (to wit, statesmen) into raising their minds to the former. It is not that statesmen do not care about keeping the peace. They are, on the contrary, well aware of its supreme importance, but they may be so well aware of it as to turn it into a truism tucked away at the back of their minds, while they work at other things.

---

* I refer to the earlier moralistic prophets, not to their post-exilic successors who were mostly narrow chauvinist nationalists of a peculiarly nasty kind.

11

Conclusion

I ventured at the beginning of this book the proposition that human history is ultimately about ideas. I have argued that the prevention of wars lies in the hands of statesmen, meaning in the hands of the men and women who constitute the governments of states. Statesmen are influenced by the prevailing moral attitudes of their times, by the existence of rules which on the whole they would rather obey than disregard, and by popular pressures which they may heed even when they dislike them. But if statesmen are to prevent a significant number of wars, they need in addition to these influences tools – and above all an international organisation with the relevant procedures, mechanisms and experience. It remains to ask how the movement of ideas contributes or may contribute to the effectiveness of international organisation for peace.

International organisation is in itself a European idea. It is open to question how far non-Europeans – west, east and south – wish to pursue it in the form in which Europe has developed it. The states evolved in Europe (with the kingdoms of France, England and Aragon in the lead) and Europe has pioneered ideas for dealing with their mutual interests and conflicts, but the world is no longer run by Europeans – except in the questionable sense that the Americans and Russians may be treated as the legatees of segments of the European tradition. Modern diplomacy is a technique developed in Renaissance Europe and international organisation is another and not much later European device. Outside Europe international organisation and experience have been much weaker. Much of Asia and almost the whole of Africa, colonised by Europeans, have been deprived for generations of the independence which creates the need for international relationships. China, the one living civilisation equivalent in calibre to the European, has been prevented until very recently from thinking about international problems by the assumption that China is co-terminous with the civilised world.

Europe therefore almost exclusively has pioneered attempts to come to grips with the problems of international order and peace in a world divided into competitive and frequently hostile sovereignties. Until the present century it was vaguely assumed that European ventures and practices would expand from Europe to the rest of the world but this assumption pre-supposes a degree of Eurocentricity which is no longer a fact and which much of the world actively resents and rejects. European ideas flourished outside Europe, not merely because European thought was fruitful but because European power gave Europeans scope for ingenuity which was denied to others. But this conjunction of intellect and power no longer exists and there is no certainty that what Europeans began will be pursued by themselves or anybody else.

Cultures overlap but they also differ, and what marks their differences is the fact that the essence of one is no more than marginal in another. At the core of the Greco-Roman-European tradition is, first, humanism: the belief that human affairs are predominantly in the hands of human and not supernatural beings and that, among human beings, the individual ranks above the group (family, community, state). Therefore man is responsible, for his power to regulate the course of events entails a responsibility to try to do so. Secondly and in consequence, men and women are obliged to conduct public affairs as the application of reason to a segment of life. They frequently fail but when the irrational prevails over the rational the event is seen as an aberration or failure and not as the manifestation of a superior fateful power. One may, without being offensively European, suggest that this philosophy is not so well entrenched outside as within Europe – and that more's the pity. As Europe is cut down to size the internationalism which it has pioneered flags in the wider society in which European influence is no more than partial, while the Europeans themselves may well withdraw into a private and circumscribed internationalism of which the European Community is a foretaste: a re-direction and diminution of a thwarted experiment. The United States, too carelessly regarded as the natural trustee and torch-bearer of the Greco-Roman-European tradition, has not yet made up its mind whether to try to order the world by irresistible might or through international statesmanship. The Soviet Union has shown not the slightest inclination to assume the latter role and no other conceivable candidate for it is remotely European.

If the one promising route to more peace and less war is not to wilt by default, the idea of the UN must catch on more broadly and more commitedly than it has done so far and it must do so outside Europe as well as among its (too frequently dismissive) European progenitors. But how do ideas change? What makes people change their minds and their ways?

It is comparatively easy to agree in retrospect that round about such-and-such a time such-and-such a change took place; but why it did so is perennially debateable. There is some truth is the view that a Great Man or Teacher changes the way people think: Socrates perhaps, or Copernicus or Descartes or Freud. Yet a backward glance over any large stretch of history reveals how impossible it is to equate an era with one man, however extraordinary his powers of argument or revelation: the Enlightenment, for example, is greater than Voltaire (or anybody else) and it would be ludicrous to maintain either that Voltaire started it or that without him it would never have been. However epitomised, changes are wrought at a more general level and therefore either by emotions or intellectually. An active educational system, the free play of brainpower, makes for a certain kind of change, particularly the kind called progress. The impact of external events changes people by making them optimistic or fearful. Disasters like the Wars of Religion in Europe and the Thirty Years War have often been cited as instances of excesses which turned stomachs and minds and the same claim has been made for more recent catastrophes: the massacres on the western front in the First World War and the mass bombing of the Second. The Black Death is a more persuasive example, more shocking because it was at the time more inexplicable and uncontrollable than any war. This scourge happened to appear in Italy at a time when the principal republics were already depressed by economic collapse, occasioned particularly by over-ambitious and over-expensive foreign policies (a form of greed which incidentally was also a precipitating cause of the French Revolution). This concatenation of catastrophes, embracing the mysterious as well as the known, produced effects which may be studied in the record since they are literally visible in the changes wrought in the visual arts and literature of the fourteenth century.* The humanity and domesticity evident in the work of Giotto and Duccio and their immediate followers in Florence and Siena in the first part of the century were replaced by an abrupt shift in both style and subject matter as painters and their patrons, reflecting the changed values imposed by disaster and fear, preferred to portray the awful power of a supernatural god, the devout supplications of his creatures and the saving authority of an ineffably dominant church. This change in temper is ever more dramatically manifested in that examplar of the age, Boccaccio. Boccaccio began writing his *Decameron* in the year when the plague arrived but (except in his preface) he neither mentions it nor appears touched by the shakes and quakes which assailed his contemporaries as they faced the prospect of eternal damnation in retribution for the sins which had brought the plague upon them. Yet a few years later Boccaccio too was struck and by the time when he came to write his *Corbaccio* this debonair gentleman and humanist was obsessed by the moral emptiness of his society, was disgusted by sex and women and regarded even literature as a distraction from the call to ceaseless devotion. His entire climate had changed and so had he – and countless others of his age.

Analogies, however proverbially riddled with pitfalls, are useful. This medieval illustration suggests that calamities change ideas, not irreversibly (that seems impossible) but deeply and for quite a long time. In Europe in the fourteenth

---

* See Millard Meiss, *Painting in Florence and Siena in the Fourteenth Century*, to which I am indebted in this paragraph.

century a combination of misfortunes, of which the plague was the worst but not the only one, shifted men's minds from the human to the superhuman, from a human order whose main cement was the rights of individuals secured by social bonds and by law, to a divine order beyond human understanding and control and regulated largely by fear. The two orders are not mutually exclusive but a society dominated by the one rather than the other weighs its concerns differently, and whatever value judgements may be made for or against either order it is evident that the one will handle its affairs differently from the other. No man can give equally urgent attention to his own salvation, body or soul, on the one hand and his relations with his fellows on the other.

One consequence of the apocalyptic horrors of the fourteenth century was to undermine an idea which had played – and was later again to play – an exceptional role in western civilisation. This is the idea that a man of consequence owes something to his fellows. In classical Athens and other ancient Greek democracies a man of wealth and status was expected to give time and service to his city, to perform civic functions *gratis* or give money for ceremonials or the city's defences. The Roman class cherished the same notion that wealth and eminence required a man to assume, and deserve, public office and to discharge it for the common weal. The medieval feudal contract and the medieval idea of *noblesse oblige* were similar: by the feudal contract the vassal owed services and in return the lord owed protection, forfeiting the services if the protection were not provided. To such ideas it is often tempting and always easy to pay no more than lip service, but even lip service attests the existence and vitality of the idea.

Modern centuries have seen a recrudescence of this idea of service but it is once more threatened as it was six hundred years ago. The principal threats are two and the consequences could include – appear already to be entailing – a slide into an anarchic and therefore more bellicose state of affairs.

The first thing is the onset of a sense of doom analogous to the unmanageable fears raised in the fourteenth century by economic insecurity, plague and fears of divine displeasure. The present century has produced two terrible and sickening wars and, as soon as the second of these ended, the dangerous mysteries of nuclear power. The possible use of nuclear weapons entailing world-wide calamity, the growing fear that the peaceable generation of nuclear energy is also hazardous in the extreme, and the uneasy suspicion that governments and scientific establishments know less than they say they know (and a lot less than they are willing to tell) about the control of nuclear poisons – all these things cause deep disquiet which, by troubling the minds of men and sharpening their tempers, detracts from the rational pursuit of a humane and secure society.

But it is a mistake to over-emphasise any one element in a society and it is a peculiarly easy mistake to focus on what is new and dramatic. The second threat to the Greco-Roman idea of service is less obvious but more deeply embedded. It is economic (and again the analogy with the fourteenth century obtrudes itself). The critical decline in the older industrial societies of western capitalism has become a commonplace of contemporary debate and its various components – particularly in the British case – have been examined many times. But more important than the decline of a particular industrial economy is what has taken its place, for the crucial shift is not from one centre of industry to another but the displacement of one kind of capitalism by another, of industrial capitalism by financial capitalism. It is the latter rather than deficiencies in the former which constitutes the unacceptable face of capitalism.

Politically the shift is important because it creates a new elite with different ideas. There always are elites (to attack the concept of elites is a waste of breath); what matters is how the ruling elite thinks. Industrial capitalism had a decent injection of the idea of service, inherited from Greece and Rome via the feudal contract, so that the aggrandizement of the industrialist and of the rising middle classes as a whole was tempered by the idea that success entailed obligations. These might be discharged by greater or smaller acts of charity, or they might be sidestepped altogether, but whether honoured or not they were felt to exist: they were a factor in the ideology of a new elite whose wealth and power entailed some public service. Furthermore, the industrialist made things which, almost by definition, other people wanted. So other people counted.

This is not true of the financier, the man who makes not things but money. What the industrialist makes is either well or ill made; but money is just money which can be measured only in quantity, not in quality. Typified by the heroes of American soap operas, by their real-life counterparts in Texas and California and by their would-be imitators all over the world, the modern financier is culturally far removed from the hard but extraverted heroes of nineteenth-century capitalism with their sense of responsibility. And, even more than his predecessors, this money-maker and money-lender shapes, through immense and laudatory publicity, the ideas of the new capitalism and so of the societies which it dominates. This is not an American perversion of a more decent European tradition: its seeds can be seen in Balzac's financiers, the baron de Nucingen for example, whose peers were every bit as vicious and selfish as any modern billionaire. What has happened is a shift of economic power with a corresponding shift in values and ideas, as the very word capital had altered its meaning from (mainly) stocks and establishments and skills to (mainly) money.

This newest elite uses money as the major measure of virtue. One political consequence has been an obsessive, frequently half-baked concern with that part of economic doctrine called monetarism.* Secondly, a money elite uses financial profitability as the sole criterion of success, even when that profitability is reached by sacking people – often an uneconomic proceeding – and so excluding them from the economy which is then declared to be mended. And with this outlook goes, first, an indifference towards, or at least an unpleasing equanimity in the face of, human calamities; and secondly, a derogation from the rights of individuals secured by law. The governing elite in a money society reduces the functions of government to keeping the books

---

* Monetarism, like all branches of economic theory, puts the emphasis in economics in one place rather than another. It provides matter for economic argument. Its political applications, whether Reaganite or Thatcherite – and they are not the same – are forms of economic illiteracy derived from political ideology.

and keeping public order (very necessary but far from all-embracing matters) and making life easier for money-makers in the belief that their prosperity is a sufficient key to the creation of wealth and its dissemination.

This outlook is replicated in international affairs – the same calculation of crude gain, corporate or national: the same denigration of rules and legalities which get in the way: the same flight from reason at the slightest prompting of immediate emotions: the same shrinking of vision. All these are human failings which flirt with disaster. In the extreme instance of the American attack on Libya Gadafi was not judged to be a criminal but was proclaimed to be one (which he may well have been); evidence against him was produced only *ex post facto*, was submitted to no established judicial or even political tribunal, and was garbled in translation. Some things may be achieved this way but peace is not one of them. On the contrary, an act of violence which killed two people was taken to justify a much greater act of violence, a crime was answered by an act of war. A very bad example was set – and was quickly followed by President Botha's simultaneous acts of aggression against three of his neighbours.

There are counter-currents. They seem at present weaker, but two – one new, the other renewed – point towards a more orderly world regulated by something better than the truncheon. The new idea is summed up in the colloquialism: You cannot win. This loose phrase has suddenly seemed to make sense. But it is far from being widespread. Even a war like the Second World War may be judged more gainful than the opposite if you put in the scale of its successes the destruction of nazi evils; and outside the range of Superpower conflicts war is far from being written off as senseless or useless. Try telling Khomeini's followers that war is futile. There are more people like them in the world than there are campaigners against nuclear weapons.

The second change in the climate of opinion about international violence and war is the reversion, again far from widespread but nevertheless discernible, to the medieval notion that war is punitive rather than an instrument of natural competition. This is partly the high moral tone of hypocrisy, invoking divine or other blessings on a thoroughly selfish operation, but there is too a genuine desire to justify a war in terms of a broad humanity rather than *Realpolitik*, to give it the policeman's cloak rather than the Field Marshall's plumes. Nyerere would have been widely applauded if he had boldly presented his overthrow of Idi Amin as a punitive expedition; the partisans of the Falklands war claimed, whether convincingly or not, that the British armada was an instrument of retribution, not gain. Such shifts in opinion are encouraging but also slow and still modest. In the short term their practical effect is small and has no great impact either on the thinking of statesmen or on the current development of international organisations; but in the long run they undermine the state's claim to a monopoly of legitimate belligerence, since wars by the state are too obviously wars for the benefit of the state. The legitimate use of violence is cautiously shifted from the state to something other than the state and Article 2 of the UN Charter is reinforced.

II

There is peace and there are wars. This asymmetrical antithesis – a singular and a plural – is telling. Peace is a state of affairs. Wars are occurrences. Each war has its own circumstances and causes. There is therefore no formula for securing Universal or Perpetual Peace and the search for such a panacea is a misdirection of effort. It is utopian and Utopia is Nowhere – Erewhon.

But if war cannot be abolished, wars may be prevented. Weapons, Simone Weil wrote, do not go off by themselves. There has to be a human agent and the agent who can start a war may prevent one. This is hard work requiring persistence, sense and imagination, backed by organisation and experience: almost a new professionalism but one with roots in traditional statesmanship and diplomacy.

The burden of the arguments advanced in this book is that the prevention of wars lies chiefly, even overwhelmingly, in the hands of the men and women who direct and govern states, who have a duty to prevent these states from coming to blows, and who need standing machinery to support them in this task. Without these aids they are the more likely to fumble and to be reduced to desparate measures taken tardily in a crisis whose outcome will then depend more on luck than anything else. The history of international contacts and conflicts, and of international organisations, over the centuries has been a gradual response to the realisation that these propositions are true. To put it more briefly: the UN, like its predecessor the League of Nations, is on the right and only track if the number of wars in the world is to be minimized. And since the UN is an idea harnessed to an organisation its success depends on those who collectively go there and individually work the machine or refuse to.

The main threat to peace is not the existence of weapons but the behaviour of those who have them. This does not mean that we have to wait for an outbreak of amity between the Superpowers or other sets of adversaries – which is in any case extremely unlikely. Distrust, amounting at intervals to acute hostility and fear, is part of the state of affairs with which statesmen have to be prepared to cope and without which they would not be much needed. Wishing this hostility away is vain; and supposing that in the absence of amity nothing can be done to make the world function sanely is stultifying.

Vast national armouries are terrifying. The effects of using them cannot be assessed but must be terrible. How the weapons will work, and whether mankind will survive their use, are questions which cannot be answered without having a war – and so, being unanswerable, not worth asking.

The number of nuclear warheads in the world may be decreased by agreement among those who have them. That would be a sensible thing to do, if only because the possession of anything to excess is pointless. The complete elimination of nuclear weapons is not impossible but it too is extremely unlikely: the one likely occasion for their elimination is the invention of other weapons of at least equivalent effectiveness. In terms of peace therefore the elimination of nuclear weapons is a side issue.

General disarmament on a massive scale is also extremely unlikely. It would certainly reduce the damage which a war would do but it would not by itself reduce the causes of war or their incidence. It might even make war more palatable than it is at present. General disarmament, a seductive notion in the 1950s which came to a predictable nothing, is one of those grandiose visions which get in the way of more modest but more productive aspirations.

For it is a mistake to suppose that spectacular dangers call for spectacular counter-measures. The prime requirements for the prevention of wars are unspectacular: they are sanity and patience. Unlike amity, which is a relationship, these are qualities which can be independently cultivated on each side of any fence or curtain and, again unlike the search for amity, they can exist in any situation. One of the surest ways to get a war is to assume that the other side does not have them. Patience may indeed wear thin but insanity is rare and statesmen verging on insanity are usually removed by their own scared colleagues.

All this may seem a long way from pacifism – from the Sermon on the Mount, the Quakers and the Mennonites, the modern apostles of non-violence such as Tolstoy or Gandhi. But it is not. It is on the contrary the logical and practical way of implementing that most compelling ideal.

This war or that may be averted by luck or aborted by accident, but that is not a very consoling thought. The principal positive way of averting war has been diplomacy *ad hoc* which, as the record shows, is inadequate. Significantly to reduce the incidence of war requires a system, with rules, within which to work at the business of stopping a war before it begins or very soon after. The UN is such a system and it has two considerable virtues: it is an improvement on previous systems and it exists. It has also defects which are even more evident than its virtues and have been aggravated in the last couple of decades by the scepticism, narrowness and perplexities of national leaders, and also by incomprehension.

The demotion of the UN has been due in no small measure to its failure to do things which it is not designed to do and which are in any case impossible. First, it is absurd to expect war to be totally eliminated because this will not happen. Secondly, it is useless to try to get major nuclear powers to abandon nuclear weapons: these weapons cannot be made to disappear and will not be dropped until something more lethal takes their place. Thirdly, it is a mistake to pay more attention to arms control and disarmament than to monitoring the causes of war between particular states and taking steps to settle these conflicts before they turn violent. Finally, it is an even more chilling mistake to imagine that the strong arm above the law is superior to the rule of law as a way of reducing violence in international affairs.

There is, however, a grave and weighty proviso to the advocacy of an international system as the first recourse in reducing war in the world. Any international system is an artificial human construct and it may function effectively only in so far as it corresponds to something natural behind the system – in fact, to an international community which the system reflects. If there is no such community, the system exists in a vacuum and is useless.

A community is a vaguer and more complex entity than a system. An international community pre-supposes multiple membership; it is therefore the opposite of anything like world government (a notion as alarming as it is, fortunately, impossible). It pre-supposes shared values as well as shared interests, interacting with divergent ones but on the assumption that the divergences should be subordinated to the commonalty. It pre-supposes, finally, mechanisms to achieve and embody this vision and this balance, of which mechanisms the most potent and intelligible is the rule of law. It does not abjure the use of force but it seeks to control it and to keep it in deep reserve.

The UN is an international system but not in itself a community and the events of the last thirty or so years have sapped belief in the existence of an international community. The UN is a human artefact and, more particularly, a European one. It is therefore strange to many other sections of the potential international community, suspect and even liable to be rejected to the point where the rejection negates the community. This is an historical phenomenon arising out of Europe's historical role in the world as conquerer and exploiter, but also a phenomenon of a special nature because of colour. The enlargement of the community of states by the creation of a hundred new ones, together with the fact that this enlargement has been achieved by combating white supremacy, has called in question – at least for a generation or two – the very existence of an international community. About the outcome it is unwise to be dogmatic, but it is possible to maintain that of the two disruptive elements introduced by the turn of global events in this century the one is temporary and the other has been exaggerated.

The two elements are colour prejudice and hostility on the one hand and, on the other, the attempt to universalise a specifically European tradition. The latter is perhaps a less intractable problem than it seems at first sight, for although the UN and its (regional) counterparts derive from a particular tradition there is no opposing form of internationalism, no challenge from other quarters and no serious move away from the UN. Some new members had some reservations upon first joining and some still have differing orders of priorities in their approaches to the international agenda, but the damage to the UN in recent years has not come from these new members. As for the obstacle of colour, it has proved easier to overcome at the international level than within many states. Even South Africa, once a formidable exception to this comfortable judgement, has been losing its disruptive power as even white states become more concerned to see an end to *apartheid* than to defend the South African regime; and it is only necessary to spend a little time at the UN to observe how little the colour bar operates in international affairs outside the tip of the African continent. The idea of a war in which states take sides by colour is absurd.

There is therefore an international community which, in spite of its discrepancies, is becoming more coherent, and since there is an international community there is a place for an effective international system. And even if some members believe that preventing wars is not necessarily the most important single task of an international organisation, none denies that it is an exceedingly important one. All of which puts the system in business as, among other things, an organisation for the prevention of war in which endeavour it is, worldwide, unique.

III

To conclude:

The case for concentrating the effort to prevent wars on international co-operation and the rule of law is that, to borrow a phrase, there is no alternative. Brute force – something like the *pax romana* – is impossible in a world where there are two or more states with overwhelming power: they will rarely agree on when or how to use it. It is true that some wars may be evaded because war, although it is frequently successful in achieving a limited purpose, is a crude way of doing so and indiscriminatingly cruel and destructive. There is therefore a moral revulsion against going to war, just as there is also considerable difficulty in practice in calculating whether the attainment of the purpose may not be outweighed by other and adverse consequences, but wars evaded for this last reason are no more than wars postponed. The animosity or dispute which prompted the recourse to war is not removed. The contestants wait for the balance of probabilities to shift. At best there may be an interval during which something else may be done to eliminate the particular dispute. But what is that something? It is not disarmament: first, because disarmament has little bearing on attitudes; animosities do not go up and down commensurately with the stockpiles of arms. Disarmament

may alter the military balance between contestants or mutually reduce the level of their capacities, but it does not remove
grievances. Secondly, and more to the point, there is no
prospect of extensive disarmament and less than no prospect
of what is vaguely called general disarmament. We live in
an armed world and will continue to do so for foreseeable
time. Even nuclear disarmament is a will o' the wisp, for
even if one or two states were to decide to forego or abandon
nuclear weapons, it is unlikely to the point of incredibility
that those major states with the requisite technical and economic strength will renounce nuclear arms until they discover
other weapons which better serve the purpose at present
served by nuclear armouries. They may – mainly for economic reasons – reduce their nuclear stockpiles or even curtail
their research but they will not, in a nuclear world, go back
to living in a non-nuclear one.

Yet further: while it is impossible to demonstrate that the
absence of a major war – or any war between major states
– between 1945 and the present day may be ascribed to the
existence of nuclear weapons; or that, without those
weapons, the world might not have been spared whatever
it has been spared; it is nevertheless perverse not to regard
the existence of nuclear weapons as a deterrent which has
contributed something to this comparatively peaceful record.
This is an additional reason for asserting that states with
nuclear weapons will not lay them aside.

These arguments do not lead to the conclusion that peace
movements have been misguided or useless. War has
remained endemic and has become ever more frightful
without the assistance of nuclear weapons. So far from being
wrong, peace movements have most of the time been right.
They are wrong when they waste time campaigning for
things which will not happen, such as general disarmament
or the abandonment of nuclear weapons by the Superpowers.
But they are right when they urge reductions in uselessly
overblown armouries and pour scorn on governments which
spend billions on overkill. Agreements for the limitation of
armaments may not significantly diminish the incidence of
war but they are highly desirable on financial and social
grounds and probably have some symbolic or psychological
effect on the way adversaries see one another and behave

towards one another. Where peace movements are open to criticism is in their preference for disarmament and arms control over the less glamorous issues of maintaining the rule of law and supporting the institutions devoted to making it more effective.

The struggle for peace is a struggle to stem or preempt the lawlessness which leads to wars. In this struggle the UN is central. It has two aspects: as an organisation and as a body of law, through its standing bodies and through its Charter. As an organisation the UN has many faults and weaknesses; but the Charter is a substantial and positive chunk of current international law and includes the epoch-making obligation on all its members not to go to war. UN members have a choice between underscoring the weak-nesses of the organisation or, on the other hand, upholding the rules of the Charter and so strengthening the rule of law. Much depends on which choice the stronger members make. While there is nothing sacrosanct about the organisation, the Charter is a pact which must in the interests of (abstractly) peace and (concretely) member states and their citizens be honoured.

The central issue is the behaviour of states, through their governments: more precisely, it is the question whether or not states will, on a particular occasion, resort illegally to war to settle a dispute or achieve a purpose. For centuries rules and mechanisms have been elaborated to assist the settlement of disputes without war, culminating in the prohibition by the UN Charter of the use of war by the state – a prohibition which may well be said to be ahead of its time but which has nevertheless been freely adopted by nearly all the states in the world. (It is in the nature of a provision of this kind that it has to be ahead of its time and it is none the less essential for that.)

In this century these rules and mechanisms have been greatly reinforced by an enormous increase in the opportuni-ties for international communication and co-operation. This increase, which is one of the wonders of the twentieth century, has come about, first, through the techniques which have revolutionised communication so that states have no difficulty in getting in touch with one another; secondly, through intelligence-gathering techniques which enable

governments to know much more reliably what is really –
not just supposedly – happening beyond their borders; and,
thirdly, through the spread of the habit of co-operation
which has become second nature where it was hitherto
merely sporadic and inept. The day-to-day and week-to-
week routine of standing groups at the UN and dozens of
other international bodies have transformed the nature of
international co-existence. What the world sees of these
bodies are exhibitions of self-interest by visiting statesmen
in search of acclaim and justification; the reality is a much
less newsworthy but more fruitful intercourse between
permanent representatives of states continuously rubbing
shoulders with one another.

This community and co-operation rests on law. They are
unimaginable without the framework provided by the law
of the Charter and similar documents and by general international law. Like other kinds of law, international law does
not always give the individual person or state what it wants.
But the rule of law is too valuable to be abandoned when it
does not. The flouting of the law, particularly by the mighty,
is far more dangerous than the mere existence of piles of
weapons of whatever kind. It is a creeping erosion of the
world's one concrete dam against international violence and
war.

INDEX